STRUCTURAL FUNDS: GROWTH, EMPLOYMENT AND THE ENVIRONMENT

STRUCTURAL FUNDS: GROWTH, EMPLOYMENT AND THE ENVIRONMENT

Modelling and Forecasting the Greek Economy

by

Nicos Christodoulakis
Athens University of Economics

and

Sarantis Kalyvitis
Athens University of Ecomomics

KLUWER ACADEMIC PUBLISHERS
Boston / Dordrecht / London

Distributors for North, Central and South America:
Kluwer Academic Publishers
101 Philip Drive
Assinippi Park
Norwell, Massachusetts 02061 USA
Telephone (781) 871-6600
Fax (781) 871-6528
E-Mail <kluwer@wkap.com>

Distributors for all other countries:
Kluwer Academic Publishers Group
Distribution Centre
Post Office Box 322
3300 AH Dordrecht, THE NETHERLANDS
Telephone 31 78 6392 392
Fax 31 78 6546 474
E-Mail <orderdept@wkap.nl>

Electronic Services <http://www.wkap.nl>

Library of Congress Cataloging-in-Publication Data
Christodoulakis, N.M. (Nicos M.)
Structural funds: growth, employment, and the environment;: modelling and forecasting the Greek economy / by Nicos Christodoulakis and Sarantis Kalyvitis.
p.cm.
Includes bibliographical references and index.
ISBN 0-7923-7999-3
1. Sustainable development--Greece. 2. Industrial promotion--Greece. 3. Structural adjustment (Economic policy)--Greece. 4. European Union countries--Economic conditions--Regional disparities. I. Kalyvitis, Sarantis. II. Title.

HC300.E5 C48 2000
338.91'40495--dc21 00-045617

Printed on acid-free paper.

Printed in the United States of America

Contents

LIST OF BOXES

LIST OF FIGURES

LIST OF TABLES

PREFACE

The purpose of this book is to provide an analytical and modelling framework for the assessing of the effects that the Structural Funds provided by the European Union are likely to have on the economy of Greece in the short and medium run. Structural funds are channelled to Greece mainly through the Community Support Framework (CSF) of the European Union and, to a lesser extent, through the Cohesion Fund, with the main purpose of financing infrastructural projects.

The Greek CSF is designed to finance large-scale development projects and investment in physical and human capital, aiming to gear the economy onto a sustainable path of growth and prosperity. The second CSF is operational during 1994-2000 and is substantially more extensive in actions and far-reaching in impact than the first CSF that has been implemented in 1989-93. As for the other main recipient countries of European Union (EU), namely Ireland, Portugal and Spain, such an intervention has been deemed necessary in order to assist these less-developed members of the Union to modernise their economies, foster growth and approach the welfare and efficiency of the more developed members.

This process of *real* convergence is viewed as a prerequisite for the economic and social cohesion of EU, and is viewed equally critical with the *nominal* convergence objective of the Maastricht Treaty in the way of creating the Economic and Monetary Union (EMU). Per capita income in Greece was in the beginning of the 1990s less than 60% of the EU average. Unless a strong growth differential were achieved for a substantial period of time in favour of Greece, the country would have risked becoming a permanent laggard in the welfare and economic developments in the Union. In the 1960s, Greece was further behind the average European per capita income, but at least its economy was growing faster and the gap was quickly reduced over time. Had the process of fast growth in Greece continued, it would have led the Greek economy to converge with the European economies (in per capita terms) shortly after the end of this century. However, in the 1970s the speed of convergence slowed down, and in the 1980s Greece was diverging from the other European economies in terms of per capita income. It is only recently, during the second half of the 1990s that Greece has overtaken the average growth pattern in the EU and, thus, the prosperity gap with the other european states started shrinking again. A substantial impetus of this growth has been transmitted through CSF actions, and it is precisely for this reason why the analysis and the understanding of its impact and potential matters for assessing the course of the Greek economy.

Naturally the first thing one needs to explain is the gradual decline of postwar growth in Greece. There is abundant evidence suggesting that the main factors of decline were the systematic fall of investment, the deterioration and inadequacy of infrastructure, and the lack of extensive training in new technologies and skills, all of them combined with the slowness of institutional reforms in critical areas of economic activity and policy. Thus, the country was not sufficiently prepared to face the lasting consequences of shocks in energy prices in the 1970s, the increasing openness to european and world competition in the 1980s and, recently, the challenges of the Single European Market.

The CSF aims precisely at assisting the country to rectify some of those structural deficiencies. The Plan of the CSF was for years negotiated between the Greek government and the European Commission, before being been approved in July 1994. It envisaged the following main interventions:

- *raise the provision and quality of public infrastructure*
- *support fixed capital formation by the private sector*
- *boost competitiveness of the production sector*
- *improve efficiency and adequacy in education and specialised training*
- *technologically modernise the civil service*
- *foster regional development*

The extent of CSF interventions amount to no less than M∈ 32,782 over a six-year period, a sum that represents an increase of 146% over the total first CSF implemented during 1989-93. The size of the Plan is so enormous, that necessitates continuous monitoring of its implementation and extensive evaluations of the outcome, both at the level of individual actions as well as at the macroeconomy. Since the Plan involves several infrastructural and horizontal interventions, spillovers to other sectors and areas of economic activity are going to be substantial.

Our main concern is to assess the impact of CSF on growth and employment, as they are rightly considered to be the most critical factors in judging the progress of a country and its *real* convergence toward the most advanced economies of EU. Their assessment requires a careful quantification of the outcome is likely to have on the industry-wide and macroeconomic level, taking into account both demand and supply side effects.

This assessment is quantified by employing a four-sector macroeconometric model for the Greek economy that portrays the main interactions between the components of demand and supply together with the effects that infrastructure building has on growth, employment and the environment. An econometric model is a useful tool for such an analysis as it describes the basic structure and interrelationships in the economy. Although macroeconomic models have been frequently criticised for reflecting the structure of the past and, therefore, are unable to capture possible breakthroughs in the future, they still provide the most extensive and consistent quantitative framework for analysing plausible developments. Such a model can generate forecasts of the alternative course that the economy would have taken with or without such a type of interventions.

Furthermore, an increasingly critical factor for the quality of growth, is the environment. Currently, there is an intense world-wide discussion on restricting polluting emissions, and various policy schemes (such as setting permission levels or imposing taxation) are considered in EU. It is therefore essential to examine how CSF is affecting the energy consumption in Greece, and what the effects of environmental taxation might be. This is taking place by integrating a model of energy demand within the sectoral model, so that all interactions are properly taken into account.

The book is organised in five chapters, which deal mainly with the policy issues, avoiding all unnecessary technical complications. The model is extensively analysed in the Appendix, while a number of figures and tables provide the qualification of the policy analysis.

Chapter 1 gives a brief account of the problems and characteristics of the Greek economy during the last 25 years, and portrays the successive phases of growth and stagnation. Attention is paid to the structure of the labour market, the mechanism of wage setting and the role of infrastructure in inducing investment. The chapter includes the most recent surge of growth that Greece is enjoying in its way to EMU, which is expected to be completed in year 2000. The issue is, of course, how the pendulum of growth does not take another swing to stagnation, and to this aim the role of upgrading and extending infrastructure is critical.

Chapter 2 investigates the effects that a publicly provided infrastructure is likely to have on the performance of the private sector. More specifically, it is established that there exists a strong positive link between infrastructure and productivity in Greece. These findings are in line with international empirical evidence, according to which public capital formation plays a crucial role in the growth process of a country.

Coming to the point, the chapter gives a synoptic discussion of the interventions offered by the Structural Funds and the CSF for Greece. The actions envisaged by CSF are consolidated to four main types of intervention, namely those aiming to raise physical infrastructure, the soft infrastructure interventions, the aid to productive investment and, finally, the group of education and training actions. By doing so, the empirical estimation of their macroeconomic effects is facilitated.

Chapter 3 describes the new model on which our assessment of CSF is based. The model contains four sectors of economic activity, namely those of agriculture, traded goods, non-traded goods and the public sector, and includes a detail system of price formation, wage setting and public finances. Employing this model, a base forecast is obtained under certain assumptions for the period 1995-2005 in order to have a benchmark of what the economy would have been without the CSF. To this end, we describe a likely course for the exogenous variables of the model, the institutional changes likely to be implemented, and the stabilisation targets that the government has adopted, regardless of CSF, in order to reduce the debt burden and qualify for the convergence criteria of the Maastricht Treaty. The model is also subjected to a number of stylised shocks in domestic and international variables, and the dynamic properties and multipliers of the economy are analysed.

Chapter 4 describes the financial flows of each category of CSF as being outlined in Chapter 2. A framework of supply-side responses to those interventions is introduced, to express the means by which infrastructure building may generate growth and raise productivity. Employing the sectoral macroeconometric model we then assess the impact of CSF actions on the Greek economy. This is taking place by constructing projections of main economic variables under the assumptions of CSF, and then comparing the outcome with the benchmark of no CSF intervention. The effects of CSF are modelled in a two-fold manner. First, the CSF flows are assumed to solely push total demand, through domestic expenditure and personal income, and this is meant to be the demand-driven scenario. Second, a boost in domestic supply is examined through the rise in sectoral productivity due to improved infrastructure, reduction of unit labour costs and increase in capital formation. The supply-side scenario is quantified by calibrating a number of parameters on productivity externalities, generated by the new infrastructure. The model is then simulated for each type of intervention and under alternative assumptions according to whether the effects are stemming from the demand side of the economy or incorporate the supply-side responses. Changes in output and productivity growth rates, the rise in employment, and the developments in prices and public finances are analysed first separately for each intervention and then for the total of CSF actions.

Chapter 5 deals with the energy sector and the environment. Environmental effects are closely linked to developments in energy demand. Special attention is recently paid to the need of decreasing of carbon dioxide (CO_2) and other 'greenhouse' emissions that primarily arise from the consumption of energy. We describe the key characteristics of energy consumption in Greece and derive estimates of energy demand for the traded, non-traded, public, and agricultural sectors. We then integrate the energy demand and the energy price system into the macroeconomic model and obtain alternative scenaria. First, we extend the base forecast to include energy demand under the same key macroeconomic assumptions adopted in Chapter 4, without any CSF interventions. Then, the demand for energy under CSF is forecasted, again according to whether it is only demand-driven or generates positive supply-side effects. The model is then subjected to a number of policy simulations which involve a rise in energy prices in the form of an energy tax under the assumption of fiscal neutrality. Based on the forecasts of energy demand, we derive the CO_2 emissions for the period up to 2012, which is the terminal year of the internationally agreed period 2008-2012 for environmental action.

In particular, we focus on changes in CO_2 emissions brought about by the CSF. One of the major CSF interventions in Greece is the introduction of natural gas to the Greek energy system, and so we examine the effects under alternative environmental scenaria that incorporate the two main features of interest: the group of actions and initiatives incorporated in the CSF and the impact of introducing natural gas in the energy sector. In general, we find that the average annual growth rates of predicted CO_2 emissions for the period 1995-2012 are higher than world forecasts. However, the implementation of the third phase of the CSF (expected to begin in 2000) will enhance flexibility and competitiveness of the Greek energy system by setting priorities for the energy sector. It is therefore expected to drive CO_2 emissions to a much lower level by the year 2012.

The *Epilogue* summarises the results of the study, discusses the main conclusions and presents a number of policy implications concerning the implementation and evaluation of CSF in recipient countries and the new prospects of the Greek economy.

ACKNOWLEDGMENT

This study grew out of the EU Project JOU2-CT92-0257 on the 'Economic and Environmental Impact of the CSF' approved in 1993 and completed in 1998. Financial support from the European Commission and the European Centre of Excellence at the Athens University of Economics is gratefully acknowledged.

The book was being written for a number of years. Parts of it were presented in seminars, while shorter versions appeared in various journals, such as *Economic Modelling*, *Economics of Planning*, *European Planning Studies*, *Energy Economics*, and the *Journal of Policy Modeling*. We have greatly benefited from comments and suggestions by referees, academic colleagues and project participants. It is important to mention A. Andrikopoulos, J. Bradley, P. Kalaitzidakis, D. Lalas, A. Michaelides, S. Pesmajoglou, N. Pittis and I. Segoura. We are also thankful to several seminar participants, especially those in the University of York, Canada, the Bank of Cyprus, Nicosia, and the OECD LINK 1999 Meeting, Athens. Finally, the authors are grateful to E. Apostolidou, E. Polyzogopoulos and H. Xanthi for valuable research assistance and useful remarks. The responsibility for any remaining errors or omissions is strictly with the authors.

Chapter 1

THE PENDULUM OF GROWTH

1. GROWTH IN POST-WAR GREECE

In the post-war period and until the late 1970s, Greece was below the european average level of per capita income, but its economy was growing at much higher rates, so that the gap was systematically shrinking; see Figure 1.1. After the devastation brought about by the Second World War and the civil war, the economy started awakening in a desperate attempt of reviving growth and fostering employment. Investors found Greece to be a country with major opportunities in traditional sectors, which could be exploited even by firms with low technological and innovative potential.

At the same time, the workforce was effectively disciplined through both the enhancement of labour supply from the agricultural sector and a brutal repression of trade union activity. Additionally, the state managed to keep an adequate level of aggregate demand, which, in combination with import barriers and factor availability, helped to maintain high levels of employment. None of these factors could have lasted *ad infinitum,* but the pendulum reached the low growth swing sooner than expected.

Figure 1.1. Output growth in Greece and the EU (average annual rate, %)

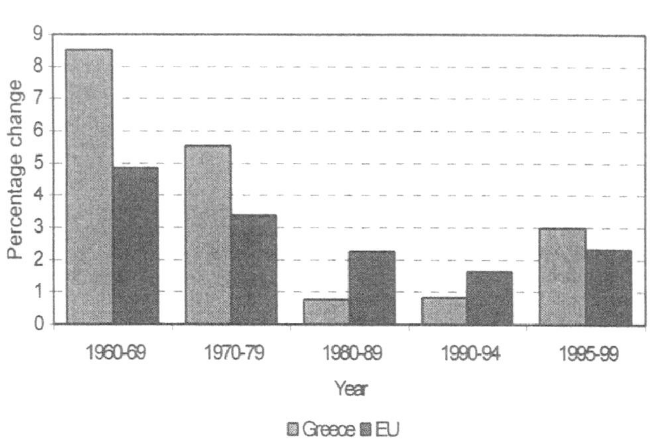

Box 1: The pendulum of convergence and divergence

During the period 1950-1972 Greece had the lowest per capita income among 16 OECD countries, but with an average rate of 6.2% per annum was ranked among the top in terms of growth. Had this process continued, it would have led the Greek economy to fully converge in per capita terms with the european economies, shortly after the year 2000.

In the 1960s, per capita GDP in Greece was growing at 7% per year against a 3.9% of the european average. With such a difference, convergence in per capita income would have taken 42 years. In the 1970s Greece had a growth rate of 3.7%, still outperforming the european average of 2%, but this time convergence would have required a period of 81 years.

In the 1980s the process was reversed and Greek per capita GDP was barely growing at 1% per annum, much lower than the european counterpart of 1.8%. Greece did not only have the lowest per capita income among these countries, but was further diverging from the rest.

In the early 1990s Greece started at last to outperform the average european growth and the prosperity gap is narrowing again (see Figure 1.2). In 1999 it reached nearly 70% of the EU average per capita income, and, if current growth differential continues, it is expected to attain the 80% convergence threshold in year 2005.

Figure 1.2. Relative index of per capita GDP in Greece (EU 15=100)

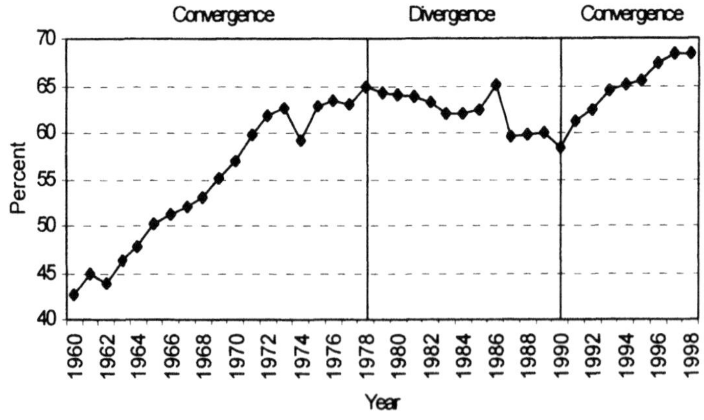

Source: European Economy (1998).

A series of events broke out in the 1970s and put an end to the development process. The oil price shocks of 1973 and 1979 meant a reorientation of world production towards more advanced technologies, the implementation of which required a much more efficient economic environment than before. Fixed capital investment became internationally scarce and started to concentrate in countries that could offer a highly skilled workforce, modern infrastructure to support the changing modes of production, and a stable institutional framework to minimise the uncertainty of expected returns.

None of these factors was readily and adequately available in Greece, and the economy entered a period of prolonged stagnation. Moreover, as the country returned to democracy in 1974, consumption soared and major institutional changes, wage-setting negotiations frequently went beyond productivity developments as a means to compensate for years of restrictive practices. The accommodative exchange rate policy did not help, while the disappearance of growth in the 1980s was accompanied by a perilous lack of fiscal discipline.

The social cost soon became acute. Unemployment was very low in the 1970s, but then started rising sharply reaching 10% in the 1990s. The stagnation of economic activity meant that new jobs were not enough for an expanding labour supply, while defensive labour market rigidities prevented firms to restructure employment. The opposite patterns of growth rate and unemployment are clearly demonstrated in Figure 1.3.

Figure 1.3. Output growth and urban unemployment rate

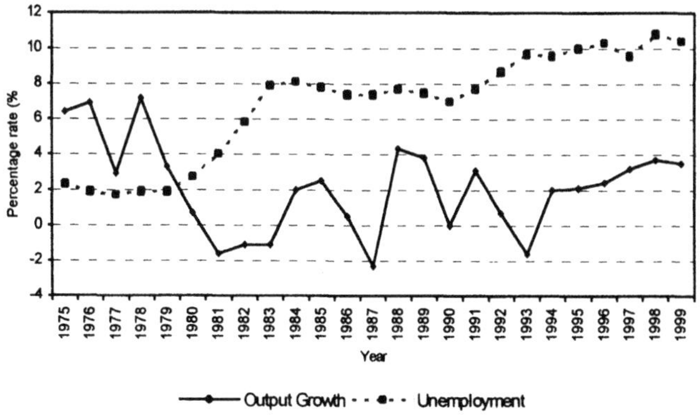

As demand-push policies were not supported by supply-side responses, it is no mystery that the lack of growth meant also a surge in prices. Greek inflation was until 1973 one of the lowest amongst OECD countries, but then jumped to unprecedented levels and remained, until 1994, the only double-digit figure in the European Union. The initial cause for the rise in inflation were the oil shocks of the 1970s that were followed by real wage increases after 1974 and, more acutely so during 1981-85. However, although wage inflation remained lower than price inflation for most of the period after 1985 (see Figure 1.4), inflation did not fall significantly until recently. Other factors such as low productivity, lack of new investment, and imperfect functioning of markets in conjunction with institutional rigidities have significantly contributed to the persistence of inflation.

Figure 1.4. Wage increases and consumer price inflation

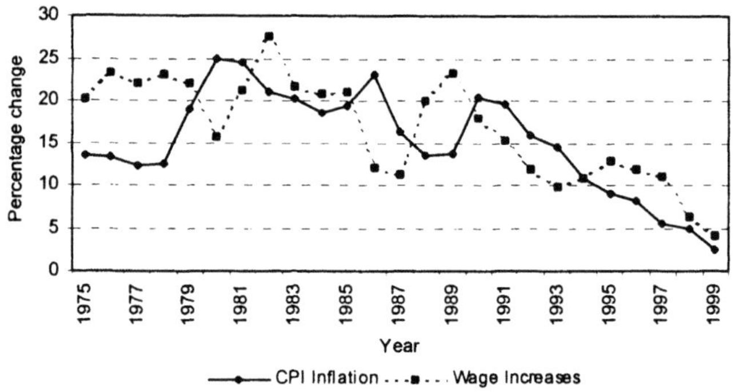

Over that period, various governments were frequently tempted to use public spending as a hedge against recession and unemployment. Predictably, the final result was a rise in budget deficits, and an exploding public debt (Figure 1.5), without any noticeable and permanent improvement in growth.

Figure 1.5. Public deficit

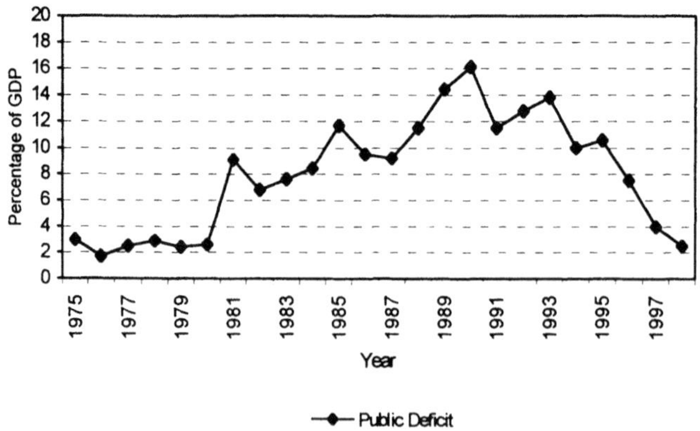

2. FEATURES OF THE GREEK ECONOMY

2.1. Sectoral Trends

Tradable sector output consists of mining and manufacturing. Its share in total output was rising during the 1960s and the early 1970s, but the process was reversed after 1975 and the share is falling steadily. Figure 1.6 shows that from one fifth of GDP in late 1970s, the share of tradable sector declined to one sixth by 1997. By analogy, non-tradable sector is constantly increasing, today exceeding half of total economic activity. Output in agriculture declined as a share of total GDP from 14.3% in 1975 to 8.5% in 1994. At the same time employment in agriculture fell from 36% of total to 18%, still much higher than european levels. Public sector involving administration, health and education activities, kept more or less the same share of total economic activity.

Figure 1.6. Share of tradable sector in total output

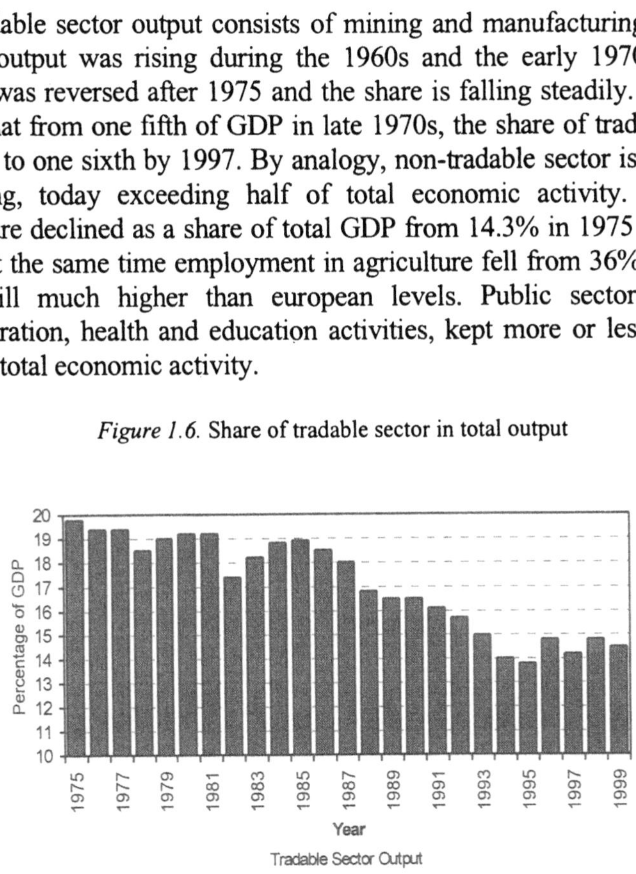

The relative shrinking of the tradable sector reflects structural deficiencies. Greek manufacturing is characterised by small productive capacity, and value-added represents only one third of sectoral output. Fixed capital investment in real terms remained until 1994 at the same level as in 1980, R&D activities are not substantially endorsed by Greek industry and the various forms of technology transfer and management innovation are limited. Despite the fact that unit labour cost has been declining in real terms since 1985, (with the exception of the politically turbulent 1989-90 period,

Figure 1.7), competitiveness did not rise sufficiently to compensate for the removal of protection brought about by the European single market.

Figure 1.7. Real unit labour costs of total economy

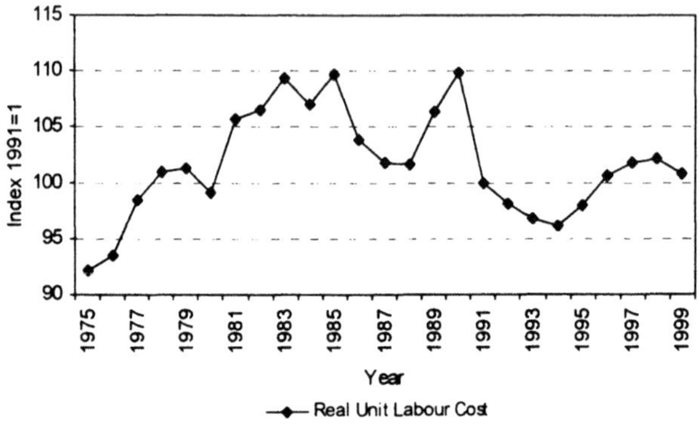

However, there is increasing evidence that in the recent years some forces in Greek manufacturing move in the opposite direction. During the last ten years, a considerable number of Greek firms managed to adopt new technologies, modernised their management and succeeded in highly competitive international markets. The relative share of tradable output ceased to decline further and industrial production started rising again with growth rates reaching 7% in 1998 and 8% in 1999.

2.2. Employment

Employment in Greece has a number of worth-noticing characteristics: First, total unemployment has increased sharply in the beginning of the 1980s and remains persistent around 10%, (Figure 1.3). One of the factors that pushed unemployment upwards, was the decision at that time to increase the minimum level of wages by 35%, as a means to compensate historical real wage losses. Implemented in a period of increasing openness to foreign competition immediately after the accession to the EU, the measure simply meant a serious fall in competitiveness. Real unit labour costs rose by 20% between 1983-80, and soon several firms -especially of medium size- were out of business. No doubt, unemployment started soaring in levels never experienced in Greece in the past, and became an intractable problem for many years.

Second, variability of employment over the business cycle is three times lower than the variability of output, suggesting the presence of strong labour hoarding practices in Greece. This implies that increases in output are translated to smaller shifts in employment.

Third, public employment is excessively high compared with depended employment in the private sector. The number of employees in the civil administration and the wider public sector was constantly rising between 1975 and 1990. Hiring was particularly high in the period after one political party was first coming to power as is clearly shown during 1975-77 after the elections of 1974, in 1982-84 after the changeover in 1981, and during 1989, when two elections took place (see Figure 1.8). This phenomenon is suggesting clientilistic practices that were finally subdued in the 1990s.

Figure 1.8. Employment growth

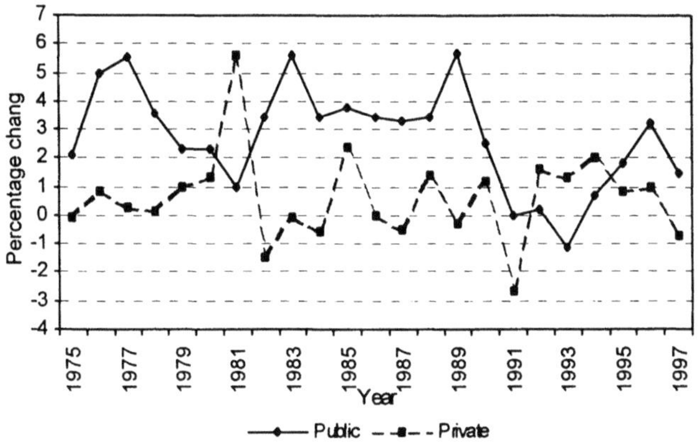

Fourth, agricultural population in Greece is trend-falling and shows considerable variation between successive periods of low and high land fertility due to the changing number of hired agrarian workers. On the other hand, self-employment is widespread and rising.

Fifth, regarding skill composition, evidence suggests that there is shortage of skilled and highly trained workforce, whilst there is abundance of unskilled labour. The situation did not seriously improve over the last decade, despite the rise in demand and the training opportunities available. According to a study (Brennan, 1993), Greece had among EU the lowest allocation of funds during the period 1989-1992 to the training of the workforce to new skills.

Employment in manufacturing has remained virtually constant during the last decade. Combined with the slightly rising output, this implies that labour productivity did not significantly increase. In contrast, employment in non-tradable sector increased less rapidly than output, reflecting a rise in average productivity.

Box 2: Unemployment: causes and policies

The issue of unemployment has become one of the key aspects of social intervention within the EU. Structural policies have attempted to offset the negative consequences of industrial restructuring by improving the education of the workforce through retraining schemes, and by generating favourable conditions for existing firms through the encouragement of new activities and job creation.

In Greece, the high growth rates observed during the last three years were not initially accompanied by a decline in unemployment; for instance, in 1997 employment *fell* by 0.5%, albeit the economy grew with an annual rate of 3%. In 1998 unemployment rose to 10.8% (compared to 9.6% in 1997) despite the rise in employment by 3%.

The main reason behind the rise in unemployment is undoubtedly the rapid increase of labour supply. This is partly due to rising female participation, domestic migration from rural to urban areas, the repatriation of Greek-speaking migrants and the legalization of foreign immigrants from the former Eastern economies. It is estimated that more than half a million workers belonging in the last two categories were added to the workforce.

A number of policy measures have attempted to face structural unemployment and labour market rigidities. These include:

- acceleration of economic growth
- removal of institutional inflexibilities
- education and training programmes for youth and long-term unemployed
- avoiding marginalisation and exclusion by ensuring access to labour opportunities

These measures have already started to operate. Unemployment fell to 10.4% in 1999 and is further expected to fall in 2000 in accordance with higher growth rates. More important, employment in the private sector is expected to increase at an annual rate of 3% compared to an annual average of 1.3% in the 1980s.

2.3. Investment And Infrastructure

Public capital accumulation in post-war Greece can be divided in two periods. From 1950 until 1973 the country experienced high accumulation rates, with an impressive average of 5% per year. Foreign investment flows, shielded by protective legislation, boosted economic growth during the 1950s. In the years until mid 1970's, investment on infrastructure reached high levels with emphasis given on transport and communications.

On the contrary, the most important characteristic of the Greek economy in the post-1974 period, was the gradual reduction of national resources allocated to investment. From 1974 until mid-1990s, the capital growth rate fell to an average rate of around 3% per year. Between 1950 and 1974 the public investment to output ratio averaged 9% and then fell to an average of 6% for the successive period 1974-1994.

One important feature of this 'regime change' was the slowdown of private investment. The corresponding figures for private investment to output ratio were 26% and 19%, respectively. Periods of rise in public infrastructure seem to be associated with increasing private investment; more significantly, when the former falls, the latter is also adjusted at a lower level. Figure 1.9 shows the development of infrastructure as a share of output during the last three decades in Greece and compares this with the share of private investment in output.

Figure 1.9. Public and private investment

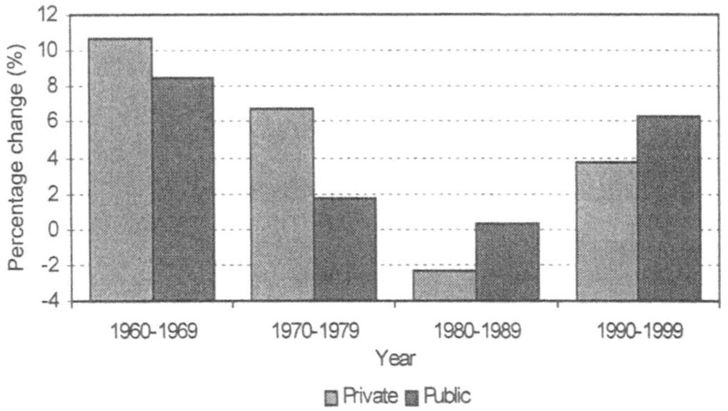

Box 3: Economic fluctuations in Greece

Another interesting aspect of growth is the analysis of aggregate economic fluctuations between peaks and troughs of economic activity. This issue has recently become particularly important regarding the viability of the European Monetary Union (EMU). The design of institutions and policies associated with such plans critically depends on the uniformity of some fundamental characteristics of the economies in question regarding preferences, the nature of technology shocks, and the underlying propagation mechanisms.

To tackle such questions for the Greek economy, one needs to decompose economic variables into trend and cyclical components and analyse the statistical properties of the latter. In Greece, peaks of economic activity occurred in 1972 and 1979, and were succeeded by troughs in 1968, 1974, 1983, 1987 and 1993 (see Figure 1.10). Peaks in the period up to 1980 are in general more pronounced and longer lasting than troughs. In contrast, for most of the period after 1980 the economy remained below potential levels.

In the beginning of the 1990s, the economy witnessed a new recession, following the general economic conditions in the EU. In 1996 the economy entered a period of prolonged growth, supported by institutional changes and financial flows from the EU.

Figure 1.10. Business cycle

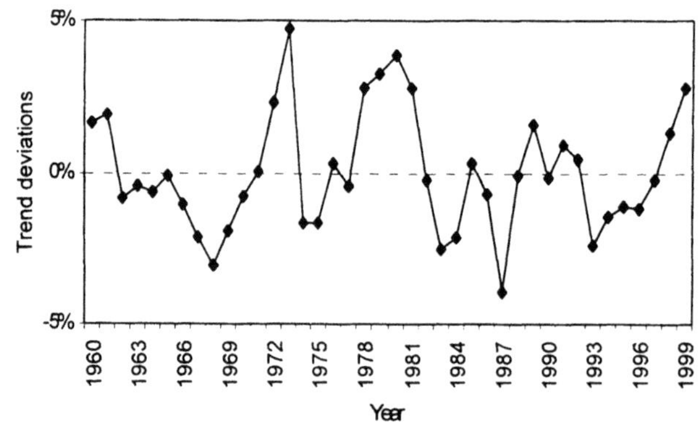

2.4. Public Finances

Public debt and deficits were generally kept under control until the late 1970s, but then entered a period of instability which was firmly corrected only in the late 1990s. Peaks in expenditure and troughs in revenues occurred mainly during the election years 1981, 1985, 1989 and 1990, pointing to the existence of strong political cycles in the Greek economy (see Christodoulakis, 1994b).

It was first the conservative government that initiated in 1980-81 the first major departure from prudent fiscal policy by increasing public spending, lowering taxation and expanding credit. The successive socialist government soon started a new round of spending increases in 1982 by raising the minimum level of wages by 35%, enlarging public employment and vastly expanding both the benefits and the number of claimants of the welfare system. Total spending of general government rose by more than 5 percentage units of GDP between 1981 and 1985 while total revenues rose at a slower rate; as a result, public deficit rose significantly (see Figures 1.5 and 1.11).

Figure 1.11. Public spending and revenues

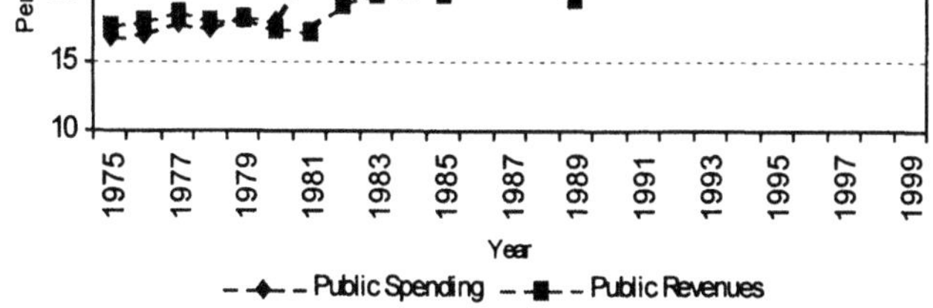

To finance its persisting deficits the government was increasingly borrowing from abroad. In 1985 foreign debt had risen to 24% of GDP, compared with 7% of GDP in 1980. An extensive stabilisation programme was called for in October 1985 with a discrete devaluation by 15% and a tough income policy that ruled out pay rises in the public and the private sector. The abandonment of the stabilisation programme in 1988 and three successive elections in 1989 and 1990 meant that no long-lasting measures could be enforced and, as a result, fiscal imbalance deteriorated further: in 1990 public debt was above 80% of GDP and accelerating, while budget deficit reached 16% of GDP. A new stabilisation plan was then introduced in 1992 that included an increase in petrol tax, reforms in the social insurance system, and a wave of hastily privatisations. Budget deficit was reduced, leading for the first time to a small –though inadequate- primary surplus. The programme had only limited success and, in any case, it was once more halted by the early elections in 1993.

In June 1994, the government submitted a new Convergence Plan to the European Commission in which it pledged to reduce public debt and deficits, bring down inflation, increase labour market flexibility and lead the country out of the conundrum of fiscal peril and the lack of growth. With a new impetus after the elections of 1996, fiscal stabilisation was, at last, started to pay off and created the conditions for low public deficits, a declining public debt and an acceleration of growth.

3. A NEW TRACK OF GROWTH

After fifteen years of fiscal expansion and economic slowdown between 1980-94, fiscal stabilisation seemed to be unattainable, and that could bar the national goal of participating in the EMU. However, the policy followed after 1994 led to a reversal of the pendulum towards high growth and fiscal stability.

Inflation fell to around 2% in the last quarter of 1999, while the EU-harmonised budget deficit reached 1.6% of GDP in 1999, much below the level required for the Euro zone. GDP grew by 3.5% in both 1998 and 1999, which is higher than the european average. Output growth moves along with a roughly 11% annual increase in total investment (14% for public investment and 9% for private investment). Over the same period the average growth rate of investment in the EU was around 4.5%. Resources from the european Structural Funds are crucially responsible for this turnaround of investment and growth. The private sector also invests heavily because profitability is high. Industry grew by 7% in 1998 and 8% in 1999 after many years of stagnation.

Public debt is still among the highest in the EU (it ranks third after Italy's and Belgium's), but is declining rapidly. As a ratio to GDP, it has fallen from 113% in 1996 and reached 104% at the end of 1999. This is the largest decline ever taken place in Greece and more than the average reduction among the EU member states in the same period. The decline is due both to the fiscal tightness and the significant privatisation revenues. Traditional factors of debt escalation, such as state guarantees for poorly serviced loans by the public sector, are now severely controlled, and public enterprises have to exhaust cost-reducing measures and fiscal restraint, before they are allowed to borrow for capital investment.

More emphasis is put on structural reform and privatisation. Due to a battery of structural measures taken in 1998, public firms are now more efficient and competitive, labour markets have become more flexible, local authorities and public institutions are more efficiently managed and better equipped, and social security is less costly. There has also been progress on the privatisation front with total proceeds accounting for 3% of GDP in 1998 and more than 2% in 1999. The long-awaiting restructuring of loss-making public corporations (mainly in the transport, post-office and defence sectors) has started. It involves the elimination of restrictive labour practices, the removal of surplus personnel to other areas and the formation of strategic alliances with domestic or foreign firms. Ongoing reforms include further privatisations and the deregulation of monopoly sectors, such as energy production and immobile telecommunications.

A number of major large-scale infrastructure projects co-financed by the EU, are already underway. Two new highways crossing the country south-north and west-east of more than 1,500 km, the new Athens airport, the modernisation of railways, the new Athens subway lines, a new pipeline that spreads the use of natural gas around the country, as well as numerous other new airport and port facilities, offer considerable opportunities to foreign investors to participate as suppliers, contractors or in project financing. The construction of large athletic, cultural and residential projects so as to host the 2004 Olympic games, will further boost economic activity.

Apart from the obvious positive effect on investment, the CSF will increase productivity and growth. The way to ensure this is by targeting sectors in which the country has a serious chance to develop an international comparative advantage, and by following certain criteria in the selection of the plans to be financed. These criteria include:

- project *viability*
- perspectives of economic *utilisation*
- *supplementarity* to each other
- *additivity* between community and national funding

All the above considerations point to the need of ensuring maximum utilisation of Structural Funds within a framework of assessing their impact under alternative assumptions about allocation and efficiency. The extent to which Structural Funds affect growth and the way to obtain quantitative estimates of such effects are extensively discussed in the following chapters.

Chapter 2

PUBLIC INFRASTRUCTURE, GROWTH AND THE COMMUNITY SUPPORT FRAMEWORK

1. THE EFFECTS OF PUBLIC INFRASTRUCTURE ON GROWTH: INTERNATIONAL EVIDENCE

The suggestion that neglecting to raise and improve infrastructure may cause a slow down of growth has attracted much attention from both the research community and policy makers alike. The link between public investment and economic activity had been first addressed analytically by Arrow and Kurz (1970). However, it was not until Ratner (1983) that a quantitative assessment was obtained for the G7 economies in association with the aggregate stock of public infrastructure invested in those countries. His findings prompted further research on the US economy and other countries.

The majority of empirical studies on various economies tend to agree that the size and quality of public infrastructure is an important determinant of productivity and economic activity. Three main approaches have been employed in the literature to examine such effects. Several studies use a production function framework for output or total factor productivity (TFP) growth, and treat public infrastructure as a factor of production.[1] Other studies use the cost function approach to estimate the impact of public capital on total cost, and derive the substitution elasticities between the factors of production. Usually, public capital is treated as a partially unpaid input in private production in the sense originally described by Meade (1952). Finally, there is also the profit function approach[2], which is used to estimate input demand and output supply elasticities with respect to public capital.

Following the first of the above approaches, Aschauer (1989) estimated a Cobb-Douglas function and established that the decline in US productivity growth in the 1980s was associated with the neglect for public infrastructure over the same period. He found that there exists a significant relationship between productivity and public capital and the elasticity implied that a

1% deterioration of infrastructure could have caused a 0.38 to 0.56% cumulative loss of output. The concept of elasticity became central, as it is convenient to contemplate how much extra output will be accumulated over a period of time due to an improvement of infrastructure by 1%.

Ford and Poret (1991) applied Aschauer's methodology to a broader set of data. Using alternative concepts to define infrastructure capital, they examined the impact of public sector capital on TFP growth in ten industrialised countries (US, Japan, Germany, France, UK, Canada, Belgium, Finland, Norway and Australia). Their 'narrow' definition included the capital stock of 'producers of government services' excluding defence, while the 'broad' definition further included capital stock in the electricity sector, gas and water supplies, transport, and communication. Neither definition included the military capital stock. Estimated with the 'narrow' definition of infrastructure, the elasticity was found to be between 0.15 (Japan, UK, Norway) and 0.70 (France). Employing the 'broad' definition, the role of infrastructure was found to be significant at the 5% level for US, Germany, Canada, Australia, France, Finland, Belgium and Japan, taking values between 0.15 (France) and 0.70 (Australia). A feature of those regressions worth noting is the significance of capacity utilisation, implying that the relationship between infrastructure and productivity is of a longer nature and not a mere characteristic of the business cycle. Ford and Poret also used cross-section data to test whether the country-specific correlation between public capital stock and TFP growth in the 1970s was only coincidence. Again the coefficient was found to be statistically significant, taking the value of 0.45 with the 'narrow' definition, and 0.48 with the 'broad' one. Finally, Otto and Voss (1994) found that for the Australian economy the estimated elasticity of public capital is in the neighbourhood of 0.40.

The importance of public capital on private sector performance was challenged by a number of authors. Holtz-Eakin (1994) estimated a production function using US state-level annual data over the period 1969-1986, and found that the most plausible estimate of the elasticity of state-output with respect to state-owned public capital is null. However, these estimates are not directly comparable to those obtained by the previously mentioned studies, since they referred to the effect of local infrastructure on local output. It is very likely that several types of infrastructure (e.g. communication, hydroelectric dams etc.) have important spillovers across regions, and thus a more aggregate measurement of the effect of public capital would seem more appropriate. Besides, variables designed to reflect state-effects might themselves be associated with the level and quality of state-wide infrastructure, thus blurring the effect stemming from the latter.

Box 4: The production function approach

Aschauer (1989) estimated a Cobb-Douglas production function for the U.S. private sector in the period 1949-1985 with the following specification:

$$lnY = lnA + \alpha lnK + \beta lnL + \gamma lnG$$

where Y is private sector output, K is private capital stock, L is labour, G is total public capital stock, and A is a scale parameter. The above equation can be subsequently augmented to include disembodied technical progress and the utilisation rate of the firms' capital stock. Assuming constant returns to scale across all three inputs, i.e. $\alpha+\beta+\gamma=1$, and introducing log-linear technical change, the equation to be estimated becomes:

$$ln(Y/K) = c + \beta(lnL/K) + \gamma(lnG/K) + \delta lnCU + \varepsilon T$$

In the above expression CU is a capacity utilisation variable, T is a deterministic time index to account for disembodied technical change and $c=lnA$. With constant returns to scale across private factors $(\alpha+\beta=1)$, but increasing returns to scale across all factors $(\alpha+\beta+\gamma>1)$, the equation becomes:

$$ln(Y/K) = c + \beta(lnL/K) + \gamma lnG + \delta lnCU + \varepsilon T$$

The above equations can be nested in the general specification:

$$ln(Y/K) = c + \theta lnK + \beta(lnL/K) + \gamma lnG + \delta lnCU + \varepsilon T$$

where $\theta=(\alpha+\beta-1)$. Estimating the last equation, Aschauer (1989) finds that factor elasticities for US are α=0.56, β=0.29, and γ=0.36, and that all of them are significant at the 5% level. Returns to scale are calculated to be 1.21, but the hypothesis of constant returns to scale across all inputs cannot be rejected at the 5% level.

Aschauer also estimated a TFP equation with a normalised level of multifactor productivity as the dependent variable. A strong positive relationship between public capital and TFP is confirmed, and the elasticity of the latter with respect to the former is found to be 0.34.

Estimated elasticities for European countries have confirmed the important impact of public capital on growth. For instance, in the case of Spain, Argimon et al. (1993) investigated the elasticity of output to public capital at the national level and found a value of 0.60, while Bajo-Rubio and Sosvilla-Rivero (1993) estimated the elasticity of private production with respect to public capital to be 0.19. Table 2.1. reviews the estimated elasticities of output productivity with respect to various measures of infrastructure. These findings prove the significant role that infrastructure formation can play in less developed European economies, but, on the other hand, the discrepancies between the estimated elasticity values leave the question on the magnitude of these effects still open.

Table 2.1. Evidence on output elasticities of infrastructure in Europe

Country (or group of countries)	*Estimated elasticity on output*
OECD economies: Canada, Finland, France, Germany, Sweden, UK and US	0.045 to 0.055
France	0.08 (regional)
Spain	0.19 (private capital) 0.21 (regional) 0.60 (national)
Sweden, 1960-88	1.66 (core infrastructure) -0.06 to 0.17 (non-military public capital)
Greece, 1959-1993	0.18 (large-scale manufacturing)

Source: Pfaehler, Hofmann and Boente (1996) and Mamatzakis (1999).

2. PUBLIC INFRASTRUCTURE IN GREECE

The effect of infrastructure in a less developed economy could well be stronger than in a more developed one, since underprovision of certain public services -such as R&D or communication systems- in the former is less likely to be compensated by private supply. In other cases, lack of adequate infrastructure may be of crucial importance for the lack of new private investment, thus resulting in prolonged periods of output stagnation.

Therefore, we attempt to examine here how gross sectoral output is affected by the provision of public infrastructure in Greece. The distinction between sectors is in principle important, because the positive spillovers from public capital formation on the economy could significantly differ across sectors; the results could provide us with an indication of differences in the effects of public infrastructure between sectors. In addition, we choose alternative measure of public capital instead of using solely the total public capital stock, which also includes capital generated by the public sector for various non-productive purposes. This should help to identify more closely the positive externality stemming from infrastructure capital to the rest of economic activity.[3]

To this extent, we set out to examine this impact in Greece by calculating correlation coefficients between sectoral output growth rate and alternative measures of public capital accumulation. We utilize annual data for the period 1964-1990 of sectoral output growth rates and sectoral capital stock series. Given that alternative measures of infrastructure may be of vital importance in explaining the effects of policies for public capital formation on output, we define *three* versions of infrastructure that capture productive effects of government capital: (i) total stock of public capital, (ii) 'broad' infrastructure, taken to include public capital in ports, railways, motor vehicles, civil aviation, roads, electricity, and communications, and (iii) 'narrow' infrastructure, defined as public capital in these sectors excluding electricity and communications. The latter two definitions are more closely to the spirit of Aschauer's original methodology.

The correlation coefficients on various definition of public capital are shown in Table 2.2 and are found to vary significantly between sectors. We also display the coefficients between output growth and lagged infrastructure, as public capital accumulation is more likely to operate on production with some delay due e.g. to adjustments costs and irreversibility in private capital. Moreover, we thus avoid potential endogeneity problems, which may appear when estimating the correlation between output growth and current capital accumulation.

The impact of public infrastructure on tradable sector output (which consists mainly of manufacturing) appears to be the largest. This sector is technologically advanced, employs the largest part of skilled labour force, has a relatively high capital to labour ratio and is, therefore, more akin to benefit from infrastructure and improved competitiveness. On the flip side, agricultural output seems to gain the smallest benefit from infrastructure formation, particularly when 'narrow' infrastructure is considered. This is not surprising, given the definition of 'broad' and 'narrow' infrastructure, which are mainly oriented to ameliorate the provision of services. Indeed, the coefficients of non-tradable and public sector output are higher, though lower than the corresponding ones for the tradable sector.

Table 2.2. Correlation coefficients of sectoral output growth and public infrastructure accumulation in Greece, 1964-1990

	Total		'Broad'		'Narrow'	
Output	Current	Lagged	Current	Lagged	Current	Lagged
Tradable	0.76	0.65	0.69	0.65	0.62	0.53
Non-tradable	0.61	0.35	0.51	0.35	0.40	0.23
Public	0.63	0.55	0.68	0.58	0.69	0.49
Agricultural	0.28	0.26	0.25	0.18	0.33	0.00

Notes: For the definition of sectoral output, see Appendix.

3. STRUCTURAL FUNDS FOR GREECE AND THE COMMUNITY SUPPORT FRAMEWORK (CSF)

Envisaging the effects that a rise in infrastructure is going to have by directly raising the output of the public sector and indirectly benefiting other parts of the economy, one could easily recognise its importance as a tool for activity-enhancing policies.

In an effort to help the 'catching-up' process of the least-developed regions and to finance investment the EU devised the CSF, which consists of the following actions:

(i) infrastructure projects in transport and communication sectors, and improvement projects of the environment

(ii) improvement in the quality of human capital through vocational training, retraining in new technologies and 'on-the-job' apprenticeship schemes

(iii) structural interventions in key areas, such as agriculture and tourism.

CSF financing takes place through the Structural Funds; their aim is to gear less developed economies onto a sustainable development course and, thus, enhance real convergence with other European economies in the road to EMU. A country is eligible to '*Objective 1*' (economic adjustment of regions whose development is lagging behind) if the average per capita output during the last three years prior the beginning of the Programme had been less than 75% of the EU average. Transfers through Structural Funds aim at addressing the main problems of the economy, i.e. inadequate capital formation, insufficient training of the labour force in new technologies, poor infrastructure and non-competitive industry.[4]

Greece experienced a significant rise of net resource transfers from the EU;[5] see Figure 2.1.

Figure 2.1. Structural Funds inflows as percent of GDP

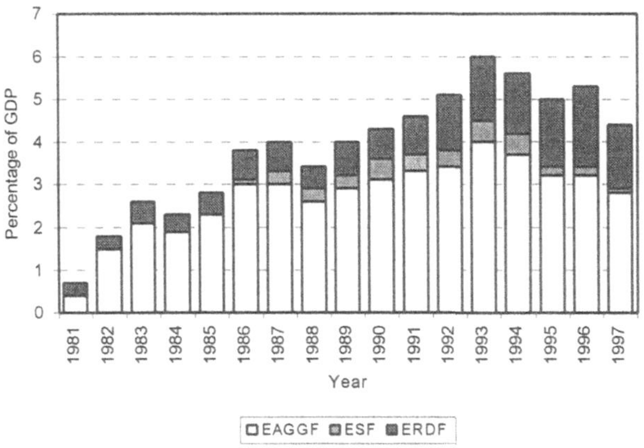

The bulk resources come from the European Agriculture Guidance and Guarantees Fund (EAGGF). In the context of the Common Agricultural Policy, Greece receives from EAGGF support for the price of the agricultural production. Having an agricultural sector of relative importance in the national economy income, the support for agriculture played an important role in the overall transfer of income from EU, especially in the 1980s. However, in the early 1990s the EU tried to contain the size of agricultural expenditure through a reform of the Common Agricultural Policy, as shown in Table 2.3. EAGGF inflows for the period 1994-99 are 10.4% of total Structural Fund inflows, which is significantly lower than the corresponding share for the 1989-93 period (19.4% of total).

Financial support for structural changes through physical and human capital accumulation has been steadily increasing over the years in three main categories: the Guidance Section of EAGGF, the European Regional Development Fund (ERDF) and the Social Fund. ERDF aims at supporting less prosperous regions of Europe through the finance of regional development projects. All of Greece is eligible for such transfers. Intervention through ERDF reached 56% of total funds for the period 1994-99, compared with 54% for the period 1989-93.

Table 2.3. Funding by Structural Funds and Cohesion Fund for Greece (in MEuro)

	EAGGF	ERDF	ESF	Cohesion Fund & FIFG	Total
1989-1993	*1505*	*4165*	*1714*	*424*	*7808*
% of total	*19%*	*54%*	*22%*	*5%*	*100%*
1994-1999	*1808*	*9837*	*3083*	*2775*	*17503*
% of total	*10%*	*56%*	*18%*	*16%*	*100%*

Source: European Commission (1997a) and CSF Secretariat, Ministry of Finance, Greece. (Notes: EAGGF denotes European Agricultural Guidance & Guarantee Fund, ERDF denotes European Regional Development Fund, ESF denotes European Social Fund and FIFG Financial Instrument for Fisheries Guidance).

Finally, the European Social Fund (ESF) aims to support less favoured groups of European society. Eligible groups are determined on a regional basis and, again, the whole of Greece is characterised as '*Objective 1*' region, that is priority candidate for such support. The share of fund inflows through ESF is expected to be 22% of total for the period 1994-99, while the corresponding figure for 1989-93 was 18%. It should not be overlooked that since 1993 Greece has also been receiving financial transfers through the Cohesion Fund. The Cohesion Fund assists projects in the environment and transport sectors; the assistance is provided directly to member states on condition that they remain within the path set by their Convergence Plan on their way to EMU.

Developments in the flows of Structural Funds to Greece can be compared to the relative flows to other EU recipient countries namely Ireland, Portugal and Spain. Table 2.4 gives a picture of the magnitude of the EU actual and planned intervention in Greece, Ireland, Portugal and Spain through Structural Funds and the Cohesion Fund during the period 1989-1999. Specifically, first CSF 1989-93 interventions amounted to 4.5% of GDP for Greece, 6% for Ireland, 6.1% for Portugal and 1.6% for Spain. Resources through Structural Funds are more than doubled for the four recipient countries during the second CSF. Assistance rises markedly to an annual average of 7.2% of GDP for Greece, 7.1% for Portugal and 3.4% for Spain while Ireland is expected to receive an amount equal to 5% of GDP annually.

Table 2.4. EU financing in peripheral countries

First Community Support Framework 1989-93

	Greece	Ireland	Portugal	Spain
EU financing (GDP %) (% of total)	2.65 (59%)	2.66 (44%)	3.07 (50%)	0.75 (48%)
Public expenditure (GDP %) (% of total)	1.49 (33%)	1.74 (29%)	1.76 (29%)	0.56 (36%)
Private expenditure (GDP %) (% of total)	0.33 (7%)	1.60 (27%)	1.32 (21%)	0.26 (16%)
Annual average (GDP %)	4.47	6.00	6.15	1.57

Second Community Support Framework 1994-99

	Greece	Ireland	Portugal	Spain
EU financing as (GDP %) (% of total)	3.67 (51%)	2.82 (57%)	3.97 (56%)	1.74 (51%)
Public expenditure (GDP %) (% of total)	1.67 (23%)	1.18 (24%)	1.58 (22%)	0.88 (26%)
Private expenditure (GDP %) (% of total)	1.86 (26%)	0.98 (20%)	1.56 (22%)	0.76 (22%)
Annual average (GDP %)	7.20	4.98	7.11	3.38

Source: European Economy (No. 65, 1998), European Commission (1997a) and World Economic Outlook (October 1998). EU financing denotes total financing via Structural Funds (European Regional Development Fund, European Social Fund, European Agriculture Guidance and Guarantees Fund and others) and the Cohesion Fund.

An important aspect of the CSF is the degree of co-financing between the EU and the national economy, with the latter consisting of both public and private investment. Regarding the first CSF implementation period, Greece received the highest proportion from the EU (about 59%) while the corresponding figures for Portugal, Spain and Ireland were 50%, 48% and 44% respectively. Inversely, the highest private co-financing ratio was in Ireland (27%) and the lowest in Greece (7%). The corresponding figures for Portugal and Spain were 21% and 16%. The public contribution was relatively the same for all four countries, ranging from 29% for Portugal to 36% for Spain.

The large disparities between the co-financing ratios in the four recipient countries are, to a large extent, eliminated in the second CSF. The EU contribution ranges between 51% (Greece) to 57% (Ireland), while the involvement of the private sector ranges between 20% (Ireland) to 26% (Greece). Consequently, there are only marginal differences in the public sector co-financing ratios between the four countries as in the case of the first CSF, but these ratios are significantly lower.s

4. AN OVERVIEW OF THE GREEK CSF

The Greek CSF for 1994-1999 has been approved in July 1994, after successfully concluding the negotiations between the European Commission and the Greek Government on the basis of a revised Regional Development Plan (RDP) that has been submitted in December 1993. The aim of the Plan was to gear the economy of Greece onto a sustainable development course and, thus, enhance real convergence with other European economies in the road to EMU.[6] The means by which the Plan aims to face these deficiencies are given by the following actions:

- raising the provision and quality of infrastructure
- supporting fixed capital formation
- boosting competitiveness of the production sectors
- improving the efficiency of education and specialised training
- modernisation of civil services
- fostering regional development

In particular, the second CSF together with the Cohesion Fund amount to MEuro 29,740 which are considerably higher than the first CSF. The CSF Plan accounts for 90% of the two, of which 25% are allocated to regional plans. In terms of financing, about MEuro 16,572 representing half of total are coming from the Community Budget, whilst the balance (44.3%) represents the national contribution, which comes from the public sector. There is envisaged to be a serious involvement of the private sector amounting to 19% of total. The co-financing from private sources concentrates on the building of physical infrastructure that can be partly operated and managed by private firms (22.3% of total), the action on competitiveness (43.8%) and in the regional plans (10.3%). There is no private sector co-financing in the Cohesion Fund, and only marginal participation in the regional plans and the interventions for improving the quality of life. Contemplating the impact that CSF is going to exert on the economy of Greece, the Plan tentatively expects that it will boost the growth rate of output by an additional 0.9% per annum, and will create around 100,000 new jobs by the end of the decade.[7]

In the early 1990's, one important issue concerning the realisation of the RDP, was the availability of the government's contribution of MEuro 7,485 given the then worrisome state of public finances. The budget was required to generate primary surpluses in order to stabilise the debt burden that appeared to be explosive over the period of implementing the Plan. The following policy dilemma emerged: either debt stabilisation by tight fiscal measures would be abandoned in the hope of a spectacular outburst of growth, or else fiscal consolidation should secure both the achievement of primary surpluses and the prompt availability of national contributions. It turned out the second option to prevail, as the Government went ahead both with the implementation of CSF and the enforcement of the austere Convergence Plan.

5. THE FIVE DEVELOPMENT AXES

The CSF Plan consists of five development axes, which are briefly described below. Table 2.5 contains the amounts allocated to each axis and the sources of finance for each of the interventions.

Table 2.5. CSF for Greece: Financial plan by axis and intervention (in MEuros)

DEVELOPMENT AXES	Total	EU	Public	Private
1. Highways and Ports	3,182	1,327	885	970
2. Railways	490	294	196	0
3. Communications	439	242	194	3
4. Energy	946	380	253	313
5. Natural gas	827	299	448	80
6. Acheloos Dam	248	149	99	0

Table 2.5. (continued)

I. INFRASTRUCTURE NETWORKS	6,132	2,691	2,075	1,366
7. Athens & Thessaloniki Tube	1,849	854	854	141
8. Health and Welfare	339	226	113	0
9. Environment	515	377	125	13
II. QUALITY OF LIFE	2,703	1,457	1,092	154
10. Industry and Services	2,809	720	468	1,621
11. R & D	579	316	106	157
12. Tourism and Culture	796	266	213	317
13. Agriculture	2,795	1,244	565	986
14. Fishery	312	150	50	112
III. COMPETITIVENESS	7,291	2,696	1,402	3,193
15. Education	1,848	1,386	462	0
16. Continuous training	1,285	756	252	277
17. Long-term unemployed	328	246	82	0
18. Civil Service	305	168	137	0
IV. HUMAN RESOURCES	3,766	2,556	933	277
V. REGIONAL PLANS	6,701	4,506	1,502	693
VI. TECHNICAL ASSISTANCE	85	64	21	0
TOTAL CSF	*26,678*	*13,970*	*7,025*	*5,683*
1. Cohesion fund – Transport	1,531	1,301	230	0
2. Cohesion fund – Environment	1,531	1,301	230	0
COHESION FUND	*3,062*	*2,602*	*460*	*0*
TOTAL CSF & COHESION FUND	**29,740**	**16,572**	**7,485**	**5,683**

Axis-I: Promotion of domestic integration by large-scale infrastructure

The first axis aims at reducing regional isolation and promoting the connectivity of different geographical areas in Greece, and between Greece and the rest of the world. Infrastructure networks are going to be built for transport, communications and energy, amounting to a total of MEuro 6,132.

In transport, interventions include the construction of major highways on the axis of Thessaloniki-Athens-Patras as well as the Egnatia Road in Northern Greece that will provide access to the Balkan countries and the Black Sea. The railway of the same axis will be modernised and connected to the Transeuropean Railway Network. Both transport initiatives will be additionally supported by the Cohesion Fund in which MEuro 1,531 are allocated to transport projects. The main networks are going to be supplemented by a number of lower-scale projects financed by actions of Axis-V for regional development.

In communications, interventions will include the modernisation of telecommunications, the expansion of networks, technological innovations and development of new products and services. Special attention will be given to building the infrastructural networks that are necessary for accessing the European networks and ensure participation in informational highways. Mail service will be restructured and modernised after a business plan is submitted describing the viability, likely extension and innovation of postal services.

Action in the energy sector will involve the completion of the natural gas mega-project, the development of energy-saving technologies, and part of the hydroelectric project in Acheloos river.

Axis-II: Improving the quality of life

Three interventions are planned by this axis involving a total of MEuro 2,703: Urban development, Health and Welfare, and the Environment. The first intervention involves the completion of the Athens underground and the construction of a similar system in Thessaloniki. The two systems are expected to relieve the two bigger cities of Greece from congestion and urban pollution, which are currently at very high levels. The second intervention includes extension and modernisation of various health facilities, the introduction of new programmes such as tele-medicine, and a national network for health and diagnostic information.

The third intervention on environment has set ambitious targets for the creation of a country-wide system for monitoring main pollutants, extensive facilities for cleaning and recycling processes, and the reduction of air pollution in the Greater Athens Area. Additionally, the plan allocates resources for the completion of the National Estate Plan, the implementation of new urban designs in decayed areas, the protection of ecological systems and the support of a system for the prevention of large-scale industrial accidents. The amount allocated to environmental actions is half a billion MEuro. However, while the Cohesion Fund will also supplement these actions by an amount of 1,531 MEuro.

Axis-III: Growth and competitiveness

The third axis constitutes the main thrust of the CSF programme that aims directly at improving competitiveness of the production sector. Of the MEuro 7,291 allocated to the axis, 38% will finance industrial investment and the provision of industry-related services. Another 43% is allocated to agriculture and fishery, while the rest will finance R&D and interventions in tourism and culture.

The Operational Plan for Industry aims to rectify structural deficiencies of the Greek secondary sector. The target is to strengthen the international competitiveness of Greek industry, as the only means to achieve a sustainable path for employment and growth. The plan envisages the inducement of foreign direct investment and the support of domestic dynamic firms as the way to overcome the chronic problems of under-investment and technological backwardness in Greek industry. The main interventions include:

- Support for the creation of new, and enlargement of existing, competitive firms on the basis of detailed business plans.
- Improvement of industrial infrastructure by a new Institute of Metrology and Standards, restructuring of management and efficiency raising in industrial zones, assistance in the implementation of environment-friendly technologies, and financing the concentration of obnoxious facilities in controlled areas.
- Boosting competitiveness of small and medium size enterprises by encouraging the adoption of new technologies, use of financial instruments and modern management.

The intervention in Research and Technology aims to improve co-operation between research institutions and firms, foster technological innovation, extend and complete the national grid of R&D facilities, and train young researchers. Despite the substantial growth over the last decade, Greece continues to have the lowest R&D expenditure as a ratio to GDP among EU countries (0.46% of GDP in 1992), while the participation of the private sector is minimal and far from being systematic. On the other hand, the research potential in Greece is growing and the country has achieved a participation rate in competitive Europe-wide programmes that by far surpasses the research population proportion of the country. The Operational Plan for Research and Technology aims at bridging the gap between a growing supply of research and a cautious demand by firms. The programme will finance large research projects specifically aiming to the realisation of new products and production methods, and will support schemes to facilitate the utilisation of existing research outcomes.

The intervention for Tourism and Culture aims at modernising tourist services in popular resorts, promote various forms of year-round tourism and support the renovation and preservation of cultural heritage. In agriculture, the intervention will assist the re-orientation of traditional cultivation, finance investment for new types of livestock and field production, and promote the rational use of local natural resources - especially irrigation systems and forests. The action on fishery includes modernisation of fishing equipment and vessels, expansion of controlled cultivation and new investment for value adding and marketing activities of the enterprises.

Axis-IV: Upgrading human capital and promotion of employment

This axis involves 14% of total CSF resources for Greece. It aims at raising the efficiency and quality of the education system, financing training and retraining of employees into new skills and technologies, helping upgrade the efficiency of civil services and implementing drastic policies to fight long-term unemployment and social exclusion. Much of the need for an expansion and modernisation of employment rests with this programme. Given that the corresponding action in the first CSF was characterised by very low returns and a widespread misuse of financial resources, special attention has been paid for the monitoring and the on-going evaluation of the programme in the new CSF. Actions will involve both training and investment in educational infrastructure, such as school buildings, computer networks and new educational tools. Cofinancing from the private sector will take place only for the actions in continuous training, since part of it is undertaken by private institutions. The remaining actions are financed exclusively by european or national public funds.

Axis-V: Reducing regional inequalities and isolation

This axis consists of 13 Regional Plans, one for every region in the country. The actions envisaged in these plans complement and supplement those included in the previous four axes. Each plan lays out a number of interventions aiming to raise the local infrastructure, assist regional activity especially in agriculture and by small and medium-sized enterprises, protect the environment and improve the social and economic conditions of the area.

6. CONSOLIDATING THE CSF ACTIONS

In this chapter we established that infrastructure has a positive long-run impact on growth in Greece. These findings confirm the international evidence that policies of public capital formation play a crucial role in the growth process of a developing country (see chapter 4). We then discussed EU intervention via Structural Funds and the CSF for Greece, which aim precisely at increasing the physical and human capital stock and put the economy on a path of sustainable growth.

The infrastructural needs of Greece seem to be so serious that, from a policy perspective, it seems better to finance infrastructure investment than to provide further pecuniary incentives for private sector investment. Moreover, given that existing estimates are derived from a static production function, it would be of particular interest to evaluate these effects in the context of the Greek economy with a full horizon perspective and examine the links between public investment and total productivity of the economy.

In such a case, economic effects stemming from the CSF may operate through the following channels. First, through demand effects which can be modelled by an increase in public investment spending, the boost in the income of trainers and trainees, and the regional or sectoral shift of demand due to the structural interventions. Second, through supply-side effects associated with a higher quality of infrastructure. These effects can be modelled by explicitly considering public capital and human capital as distinct factors of production, which accumulate according to new public investment and training respectively. Third, through crowding-out effects for national public investment, due to the fact that CSF investment may substitute away domestic funds for public projects which can then shift to consumption-oriented expenditure. Also crowding-out of private investment due to either substitution effects on firms' capital by the improved infrastructure and the labour-augmenting activities, or aggregate income effects resulting in a rise in interest rates.

To obtain an assessment of the likely macroeconomic impact of CSF its structure has to be modified, as several actions with similar expected outcomes on the economy are included in different interventions. For example, the raising of physical infrastructure is envisaged to be the exclusive aim in Axis-I, a substantial part of Axis-II (the construction of the two underground systems will absorb 68% of the resources), a small part in Axis-III, exactly half of the Cohesion Fund and an important component of the human resources programme and the regional plans. To enable the modelling of CSF, the actions entering the five development axes are grouped in four categories (summarised in Table 2.6, together with the corresponding amounts and sources of financing) as follows:

- *Type HI* (actions aiming to raise 'hard' infrastructure). This category includes the first Axis, the urban development initiative of Axis-II, the action on environment, all the Cohesion Fund, and assumes that half of the resources of the regional programmes finance physical infrastructure.

- *Type SI* (actions on raising 'soft' infrastructure): It includes the interventions on health and welfare from Axis-II, tourism and culture from Axis-III, R&D, the other half of the regional programmes, half of the human resources programme that will be devoted to educational infrastructure, and the small part of technical assistance that will finance monitoring and evaluation activities.
- *Type PR*: aid to productive investment in industry, agriculture and fishery.
- *Type ED*: half of the human resources programme used for training.

Table 2.6. Consolidated allocation and financing (in MEuros)

SECTORS	**Total**	**EU**	**Public**	**Private**
HARD INFRASTRUCTURE (HI)				
Axis 1	6,132	2,691	2,075	1,366
Athens & Thessaloniki Tube	1,849	854	854	141
Environment	515	377	125	13
Cohesion TSP	1,531	1,301	230	0
Cohesion ENV	1,531	1,301	230	0
Regional (HI)	3,351	2,253	751	347
Total HI	*14,909*	*8,777*	*4,265*	*1,867*
Percent	*100%*	*59%*	*29%*	*12%*
SOFT INFRASTRUCTURE (SI)				
Health & Welfare	339	226	113	0
Tourism and Culture	796	266	213	317
R & D	579	316	106	157
Human Resources (SI)	1,883	1,278	466	139
Regional (SI)	3,350	2,253	751	346
Technical assistance	85	64	21	0
Total SI	*7,032*	*4,403*	*1,670*	*959*
Percent	*100%*	*62%*	*24%*	*14%*

Table 2.6. (continued)

PRODUCTION AND INVESTMENT (PI)				
Industry and Services	2,809	720	468	1,621
Agriculture & Fishery	2,795	1,244	565	986
Fishery	312	150	50	112
Total PR	*5,916*	*2,114*	*1,083*	*2,719*
Percent	*100%*	*36%*	*18%*	*46%*
EDUCATION AND TRAINING (ET)				
Human Resources (ED)	1,883	1,278	467	138
Total ED	*1,883*	*1,278*	*467*	*138*
Percent	*100%*	*68%*	*25%*	*7%*
Total	**29,740**	**16,572**	**7,485**	**5,683**
Percent	**100%**	**56%**	**25%**	**19%**

Chapter 3

A NEW SECTORAL ECONOMETRIC MODEL FOR GREECE

1. WHY A NEW MODEL?

In Greece, certain studies have explored the macroeconomic impact of the CSF on the Greek economy. Capros and Karadeloglou (1989) measure the effects of the first CSF for Greece and find that the output increase is lower than the rest of the European countries, which implies that the existing disparities in growth patterns are exacerbated. Lolos and Zonzilos (1992) reach similar results. Lolos et al. (1995) use a general equilibrium model and establish that the first CSF could have raised GDP in Greece by 1.2 percent during its implementation. However, these studies concentrate on the demand effects. As a result, all positive effects are found to be temporary and cease with the end of the programme, ignoring the possibility that the investments undertaken by the CSF may accelerate growth itself.

CSF is expected to have a significant impact on both the supply and demand side of the economy. Supply-side effects stem from the improvement of factor productivity generated either as an externality through the improved infrastructure or directly by augmenting labour productivity by training. Demand-side effects are generated by the rise in the income of persons and firms involved in the implementation of CSF programs. Further, effects are also expected on other aspects of economic activity at both the aggregate and disaggregated level. The wage formation process may also be affected by the changes in demand for employment and the structure of the labour force, the capital inflow from CSF will increase credit availability in the financial sector, while the conduct of fiscal policy will also be affected through the cofinancing commitments of the Government Budget. For all the above reasons, the assessment of the economic impact of CSF should not be confined to micro-studies or benefit/cost analysis of individual projects but has also to include a macroeconomic evaluation.

Most existing models for Greece employ the traditional Keynesian framework of demand-determined output, paying less attention to supply-side effects. To various degrees, the following features tend to be underrepresented in existing macromodels:

(i) supply-side effects, by specifying an optimising framework for pricing and production decisions by firms, and an explicit mechanism for expectations formation by the private sector describing its reaction to unanticipated policy announcements and exogenous shocks

(ii) stock-flow interactions and observance of budget constraints by the government and the private sector.

Although these features are becoming increasingly standard characteristics of current econometric model building, they are hardly found in models and policy exercises for the Greek economy. Supply-side effects are only partially taken into account, and output is mainly determined by demand. Finally, the omission of stock-flow interactions leaves out important feedback between policy decisions and economic activity. For example, the task of stabilising the economy cannot be properly assessed, since long-run sustainability is ensured only if stocks-to-output ratios become finite. For instance, in the case of a rise in public spending, aggregate demand will rise but the stock of national debt will also rise. This will lead to higher interest rates to finance the debt, and to higher taxes in the future to repay it. Therefore, private investment and consumption will be at least partly crowded-out. Forward-looking agents may cause crowding-out even in the short-run. Without observing the budget constraint, Keynesian multiplier effects will underestimate the extent of crowding-out and show a strong positive effect on output.

In this chapter we present the structure of a new model that can be used for the evaluation of CSF on the Greek economy. The model consists of four sectors of economic activity, namely those of agriculture, traded goods, non-traded goods and the public sector, and includes a detail system of price formation, wage setting and public finances. Econometric estimation is carried out over the period 1974-94.

The model is then used to obtain a base forecast for period 1995-2005 under certain reasonable assumptions. These assumptions describe a likely course for the exogenous variables of the model, the institutional changes likely to be implemented, and the stabilisation targets that the government has announced to follow in order to reduce the debt burden and qualify for the convergence criteria of the Maastricht Treaty. After the base forecast is presented, the model is subjected to a number of stylised shocks in domestic and international variables, so that the dynamic properties and multipliers of the economy can be analysed.

The model includes the following features, which make it appropriate for the evaluation of CSF effects:

(i) *factor demand equations* for investment and labour are derived, which are crucial for the analysis of CSF-type structural intervention, as CSF involves large-scale investment and is expected to have a significant impact on employment.

(ii) *wealth accumulation effects* are included in the demand side, which are important because CSF is expected to generate additional disposable income for households.

(iii)*public debt targets* are incorporated in the projections of the model, thus ensuring the reduction of public deficit, and the stabilisation of public debt, which are crucial given the fiscal tightness imposed by the Maastricth Treaty.

Using these features, we construct a base scenario for the Greek economy without the effects of CSF, that incorporates a number of realistic fiscal targets and exogenous projections. This forms the basis against which alternative developments under CSF funding can be elaborated and compared. The base forecast is obtained for the period up to 2005, so that short and medium-term effects are analysed.

2. A BASE FORECAST FOR 1995-2005

2.1. Main Assumptions

In order to assess the effects that the CSF 1994-99 is going to have on the economy of Greece we first construct a base scenario that excludes this effect, although it takes into account a number of realistic policy developments and exogenous projections. Against this base, alternative developments can be elaborated and compared. The base forecast is obtained for the period until 2005, so that medium-term effects are taken into account. The starting period is 1995 so that one can compare forecasted variables with actual developments in 1995-97, where available, and get an impression of the relevance of the projections. The forecast over the years 1995-2005 is obtained under a set of realistic assumptions about exogenous variables and by considering a policy environment that is likely to prevail. The main assumptions are as follows:

Box 5: Econometric features of the model

The structure of the model broadly follows the HERMIN models which are small to medium scale macromodels of Ireland (Bradley et al., 1995c), Portugal (Modesto and Neves, 1995), and Spain (Herce and Sosvilla-Rivero, 1995). These models are designed as extensions of the HERMES models and aim at incorporating and evaluating the effects of structural policies on these economies.

The new sectoral model consists of 40 behavioural equations, 42 identities and 17 exogenous variables and is estimated over the period 1974-1994. A detailed description of model equations and identities is given in the Appendix. The year 1974 was chosen as the starting period for estimation for several reasons:

- a switch from fixed to managed exchange rates occurred in 1974
- the first oil shock in that period led to a significant and persistent rise in inflation
- the civilian government, restored in 1974, redefined the framework of economic policy by restoring free-wage bargaining, removing price controls and following a loose fiscal policy to stimulate economic activity; see Alogoskoufis (1995)
- a number of key series (such as sectoral employment) are not available before 1974

The model is estimated after taking into account the time-series properties of the variables. A battery of misspecification tests for autocorrelation, heteroscedasticity, conditional heteroscedasticity, normality of residuals, and structural stability of parameters accompany the estimates. Despite the moderate sample size (21 observations) these tests provide a reliable measure for likely problems in the specification of the equations.[8]

The series used in the present model are first tested for stationarity and, if the null hypothesis of non-stationarity is not rejected, the variables are tested for co-integration. If the co-integration hypothesis is accepted the equation is estimated in levels (long-run equation) and the residual is used as an explanatory variable (error-correction term) in the first-difference (short-run) equation. If the co-integration hypothesis is not accepted, the equation is estimated in first-difference logarithms. This procedure ensures that all parameters are consistently estimated and that reported standard errors can be used for hypothesis testing.

A1. Trend projections of exogenous variables: Variables such as the volume of world activity, population and domestically-funded public investment are set to grow at a rate similar to the moving average of the previous periods. Foreign nominal variables (world prices and unit labour cost in the EU) are set to grow at a 3% rate, close to the expected world inflation.

A2. Fixed rates and constant exogenous variables: Some policy-determined rates, such as subsidies to enterprises, transfers to households and transfers abroad, are assumed to grow at the same average rate as during the sampling period. Employment in the public sector is kept at the 1994 level. This is in line with stabilisation measures that try to reduce government spending and public employment as a proportion to total, and also with strict guidelines from European Commission to restrain public sector appointments.

A3. Exchange rate management and constant real interest rate: Throughout the forecasting period, the real interest rate on 12-month Treasury Bills is kept constant at 5% per annum. This assumption reflects the fact that capital markets in Greece are almost completely liberalised, so that monetary authorities cannot maintain a real interest rate below the world level in similar markets. In fact, the 5% level is slightly above the international real cost of borrowing to account for a risk premium due to the excessive debt burden and is very close to the actual real interest rate that prevailed in Greece during 1995. The nominal Drachma/Euro exchange is kept at the 1994 level, since a constant nominal exchange rate is a prerequisite for the entrance to Economic and Monetary Union (EMU). In fact, the Bank of Greece maintained a fixed nominal parity vis-a-vis the Euro during 1995-1997, before a fixed parity relative to the EURO was announced –after a nominal devaluation- in March 1998.

A4. Built-in stabilisation rules: The Greek economy is undergoing a stabilisation programme to harness excessive public debt and deficit and reduce the inflation rate. The main instrument of stabilisation is the increase in collected taxes, in order to achieve a primary surplus capable to reverse the otherwise explosive process of public debt. To capture this policy, we introduce a fiscal rule on the rate of direct taxation that guarantees that surplus targets are met in each period. The target for public deficit for 1995 is the actual outcome, while those for the remaining period gradually increase to the level of 1% of GDP by 1999 and remain there for the rest of the projection period. Envisaged primary surpluses will be sufficient to initially stabilise the debt-to-output ratio and then reduce it at a pace compatible with the Maastricht Treaty requirements.

A5. Increasing labour market flexibility: The government is seeking to increase flexibility in labour markets as a way to resist pressure on real pay rises and promote employment. To capture this process, we introduce a gradual reduction in the autonomous part of the wage equation by scaling down the constant by a factor φ which is equal to unity over the historical period of estimation and then declines geometrically according to $\varphi(t)=(1-\lambda)\varphi(t-1)$ over the forecasting period 1995-2005. Rate λ is set equal to 3% per annum, indicating that approximately almost one third of labour market rigidities will have been removed by year 2005. This schematic representation will be exploited later to study the effects of a quicker reform in the labour market.[9]

A6. Endogenous labour supply: The labour force in the agricultural sector follows a downward trend at the same rate as estimated in the historical period. In contrast, labour supply in the non-agricultural sector is determined through the participation rate which is hysteretic and rises with real wage increases. In the base projection, the percentage of urban non-agricultural labour force in total population depends on the real wage rate with an elasticity of 0.08.[10] This figure implies that a 10% rise in real pay will induce about 80,000 persons to seek employment.

Apart from the above assumptions, there has been no other constant adjustment of endogenous variables to bring them closer to externally discernible values. Thus, the forecasting exercise is much simplified and reveals the underlying dynamic properties of the estimated model.

2.2. The Base Scenario

A dynamic simulation of the model over the period 1995-2005, keeping the single-equation errors at zero levels, obtains the base solution. The model is found to converge quickly to solution values and to generate a reasonable outcome for the macroeconomic variables. Table 3.1 portrays the projected values of the main model variables for the period 1995-2005.

It is clear that the base scenario is characterised by a slowly rising output. The growth rate of output picks up quite closely the rate of 1995, and then it reaches a modest average rate of 1.8% over the remaining period. This rate is in agreement with most estimates of the course that the Greek economy would likely be on the following years, absent European Structural Funds or any other type of structural intervention.[11]

Given that labour market rigidities are only gradually being removed and there is no breakthrough in real wages, urban unemployment rate is persistently high. It would remain above 11% until the beginning of the next decade, and then start to decline reaching an average of 9.4% for the period 2001-2005. Total employment would rise by 1%, which is mainly due to the rise in non-agricultural jobs. At the terminal period, labour supply would have risen by 6%, due to the population increase. The base rate of growth in average labour productivity is around 1.1% per annum.

Finally, the growth rate of per capita output averages 1.1% per annum. Given that the European average of per capita output is estimated to grow at a rate of at least 1.5% in the base scenario, the Greek economy would have further drifted away from its European partners without the CSF aid.

Table 3.1. Base forecasts of key variables 1995-2005

	Impact 1995	**Average 1996-2000**	**Average 2001-2005**
Total output growth rate	1.7	1.6	2.1
Tradable sector output	1.2	2.7	3.1
Non-tradable sector output	4.4	2.4	2.7
Public Sector output	-0.4	-0.5	-0.3
Agricultural output	-4.8	0.0	0.3
Growth rate of output per capita	1.0	1.0	1.4
Total employment	-0.5	0.7	1.0
Employment in tradable sector	8.2	2.7	3.0
Employment in non-tradable sector	-2.1	1.5	1.8
Employment in agriculture	-1.9	-2.1	-2.2
Urban unemployment rate	12.1	11.4	9.4

Note: Output and employment are expressed as percentage annual changes.

3. ECONOMIC MULTIPLIERS

To portray the dynamic properties of the model over the forecasting period, we analyse the response of key macroeconomic variables to a number of separate demand and supply shocks. The numerical results for - total and sectoral- output and employment are depicted in Table 3.2.

3.1. A Rise In World Activity

The index of world activity is shocked by 1% for the period 1995-2005. The shock immediately generates a considerable increase in exports and tradable sector output. The rise in exports induces an increase in non-traded services (such as transport, communications, energy, etc.), and, consequently, a long-run rise of total output. The output multiplier is 0.3, that is of the same magnitude as in the HERMIN models for Portugal and Spain. The relevant figure for Ireland is higher (0.5) and this can be attributed to the large size of the Irish tradable sector and the more open character of the Irish economy where the sum of exports and imports reached 115.4% of GDP in 1994.

Investment in the tradable sector increases substantially while non-tradable sector investment is less affected. The immediate rise in demand combined with a slower response of supply, pushes prices up. Inflation increases in the beginning, but returns to base levels, as market equilibrium is restored. Public debt as a ratio to output is reduced, because of the higher output.[12] Unemployment rate falls in the beginning, but the rise in real wages destroys some of the newly created jobs, and finally unemployment returns to baseline.

3.2. A Rise In Foreign Prices

The variables related to foreign prices are the European price index and the average unit labour cost in the EU countries. Both of them are shocked by 10% over the period 1995-2005.

The wholesale price index is initially responding slowly, and by the end of the period it has fully accommodated the external price shock. Output deflator shows the same pass-through of the external shock, due to the sizeable foreign component in the formation of prices. The wage rate in the tradable sector rises significantly, but the increase in the real wage rate is much smaller due to the rise in domestic prices brought about by the partial transmission of the rise in foreign prices. Domestic demand rises and this causes tradable and non-tradable output to increase after a while, due to the rise in exports brought about by the less-than-full accommodation of the external shock. As a result, total output increases relative to baseline. Urban unemployment falls in the beginning, but returns to baseline as the nominal and real wage rates increase. The debt-to-output ratio improves due to the rise of inflation that reduces the ex post real interest rate.

3.3. A Sustained Increase In Public Employment

Public employment rises by 20,000 additional jobs. Since public employment is kept constant at the 1994 levels (Assumption A2), the shock amounts to an equiproportional rise of baseline public employment by 2.5%. To investigate the effects of public employment increase on public debt, the built-in stabilisation rule remains ineffective and the extra borrowing need is not offset by a tax rise.

The effect on the economy is different in the short and in the medium-run. In the beginning, the rise in public employment drives total demand upwards and increases output and employment in the tradable and non-tradable sectors. However, as unemployment falls, wages rise, competitiveness deteriorates and the initial impact on output and employment is offset. Unemployment returns to baserun level as employment in the other sectors of the economy falls. The tradable sector is most affected by the loss of competitiveness. Finally, the debt-to-output ratio initially improves since output rises, but the positive effect is gradually eroded.[13]

3.4. A Sustained Increase In Public Investment

Public investment is raised by a constant amount equal to 1% of base output in 1994. The effect of public investment in this simulation is felt through both demand and supply, as infrastructure externalities associated with public investment increase the productive capacity of the economy. In this case, all types of output increase and total output rises substantially over the baseline. Gross public deficit rises over the simulation period, reflecting the equivalent rise in public spending while the debt-to-output ratio also rises through the accumulation of deficits. Note that the built-in stabilisation rule is fixed at its baseline levels and primary surplus targets are not met, since financing the extra public investment increases government expenditure.

The multiplier (1.3) is comparable to the relevant ones for Ireland (1.2), Portugal (1.5) and Spain (1.0), reported by Bradley et al. (1995c), Modest and Neves (1995), and Herce and Sosvilla-Rivero (1995) in the HERMIN models, respectively.[14]

3.5. Increasing Labour Market Flexibility

To study the effects of a quicker implementation of labour market reforms, we raise parameter λ defined in assumption A5, from 3% to 4%. Schematically, this implies that around one third of labour market rigidities will have been removed by the end of the simulation period. The results are quite noticeable. Output rises relative to baseline and unemployment falls. Real wages are lower due to the fall of nominal wages and the gain in competitiveness is translated into a substantial increase of tradable sector output and investment.

Table 3.2. Economic multipliers

	Short-run	**Medium-run**	**Long-run**
A permanent 1% rise of world activity			
Total output	0.5	0.4	0.3
Tradable sector output	1.1	0.9	0.4
Non-tradable sector output	0.5	0.5	0.4
Agricultural output	0.0	0.0	-0.1
Total employment	0.4	0.4	0.2
Employment in tradable sector	1.1	0.9	0.3
Employment in non-tradable sector	0.5	0.4	0.3
A permanent 10% rise in foreign prices			
Total output	0.5	0.7	0.5
Tradable sector output	2.0	2.7	1.9
Non-tradable sector output	0.2	0.4	0.2
Agricultural output	0.0	0.0	-0.2
Total employment	0.5	0.6	0.4
Employment in tradable sector	2.0	2.6	1.7
Employment in non-tradable sector	0.2	0.3	0.1

Table 3.2. (continued)

A permanent rise in public employment by 20.000 persons			
Total output	0.4	0.3	0.1
Tradable sector output	0.0	-0.6	-1.1
Non-tradable sector output	0.2	0.1	0.0
Public sector output	1.3	1.8	1.9
Agricultural output	0.0	-0.1	-0.2
Total employment	0.6	0.4	0.2
Employment in tradable sector	0.0	-0.7	-1.2
Employment in non-tradable sector	0.2	0.1	-0.1
A permanent rise in public investment by 1%			
Total output	0.5	0.7	0.9
Tradable sector output	0.7	0.6	0.7
Non-tradable sector output	0.7	0.9	1.2
Agricultural output	0.4	0.7	0.8
Total employment	0.3	0.4	0.6
Employment in tradable sector	0.4	0.6	0.6
Employment in non tradable sector	0.6	0.8	1.1
Increasing labour market flexibility			
Total output	0.0	0.2	0.5
Tradable sector output	0.1	0.7	1.8
Non-tradable sector output	0.0	0.1	0.3
Public sector output	0.0	-0.2	-0.4
Agricultural output	0.0	0.1	0.3
Total employment	0.0	0.2	0.6
Employment in tradable sector	0.1	0.7	2.0
Employment in non-tradable sector	0.0	0.2	0.5

Note: Variables are expressed as percent change from base. The short- and medium run multipliers are annual averages for the first and second three-year periods respectively after the shock. The long-run multiplier is the annual average for the subsequent five-year period.

Chapter 4

THE IMPACT OF CSF ON GROWTH AND EMPLOYMENT

1. INTRODUCTION

Given the size of CSF, it is no surprise that several studies have attempted to measure the impact of Structural Funds on the economy of recipient countries. Beutel (1996) estimates that the implementation of the first CSF was associated with a significant rise of growth rates and promoted cohesion among member countries. More important, in the absence of the Plan, the gap would continue to grow and these countries would systematically continue to diverge from the rest of the EU members.

Estimates for Ireland, Spain and Portugal reported by Bradley et al. (1995a) show that infrastructure building boost by CSF will have lasting effects on the less developed regions of the EU. The authors underline the importance of externalities for the beneficial effects of Structural Fund flows during the real convergence process, although the varying degree of effectiveness depends on the particular structure of each economy and the magnitude of supply-side externalities. Gaspar and Pereira (1995) and Pereira (1997) establish that the first CSF has raised GDP in capital importing countries. Recently, Pereira (1999) investigates the effects of the second CSF in these countries and finds that the programme will reduce the divergence gap between EU and Greece, and it will only marginally improve the convergence path for Ireland, Portugal and Spain.

2. MODELLING CSF EFFECTS

CSF actions are going to influence the economy through a multitude of supply and demand effects. Demand effects are captured by the appropriate rise in the components of domestic expenditure or personal income. The supply-side effects will come by the rise in sectoral productivity due to improved infrastructure, reduction of cost due to better training of the labour force, and the increase in fixed capital formation in productive sectors as public aid will induce private investment.

The simulation results from a macroeconometric model for Greece on the effects of the CSF show that if the Plan operates only on the demand side of the economy, the positive impact during the implementation period will evaporate after the terminal period. The economy will return to the pattern of low growth that would have occurred in the absence of the Plan. In fact, given the fiscal tightness imposed by the Maastricht Treaty as a prerequisite for the entrance to the EMU, the results may even be negative for certain types of intervention, because the amount of taxation that is necessary to achieve fiscal stabilisation could have had severe distortionary effects on the productive side of the economy.

A different picture emerges when supply-side effects are incorporated in the model, which improve the productivity in each sector and the quality of human capital through:

- the rise in output growth brought about by the rise in public capital

- the reduction of real unit labour cost and the rise of effective public employment as a result of improved labour efficiency

Even with conservative values relative to the international evidence (reported in chapter 2), these supply-side effects are found to have a permanent beneficial impact on economic activity several periods after the ending of the CSF. Moreover, when supply-side effects are taken into account, the model projections are fairly close to the official estimates on the contribution of Structural Funds on the 'catching up' process of the Greek economy.

To capture and quantify the effects of CSF on the Greek economy, we take into account the diversification of CSF impact on the economy and, the aggregation of similar intervention schemes under the same category, thus avoiding unnecessary complexity, as was outlined in chapter 2. Thus, the analysis presented in this chapter will, first, attempt to shed some light on the methodology for the evaluation of CSF effects and, second, report the empirical results of the simulation exercise.

Each flow of CSF is characterised by the proportion which is expected to be implemented in period *t* and the ratios of financial contribution from EU, national authorities and the private sector, which are calculated on the basis of the amounts in Table 2.4 and 2.5. The amount of Euros allocated to a specific sector for the whole period is translated annual flows in domestic currency by taking into account

The time allocation of each type of intervention is shown in Table 4.1. The schedule depends crucially on the readiness of the economy to absorb the flows from the Union, and also on the availability of domestic financial resources. Both have improved over time, and for this reason annual flows increase during 1995-99. Still, as has happened in the first CSF, several projects are completed with some delay and final payments come after the planned horizon. To capture this predictable delay, the time factor is extended to year 2001.

Table 4.1. Intertemporal absorption ratios of CSF

Year	*1995*	*1996*	*1997*	*1998*	*1999*	*2000*	*2001*	*Total*
Time factor	12%	13%	14%	16%	17%	16%	12%	100%

3. DEMAND-SIDE EFFECTS

Each flow is modelled in such a way as to reflect both the increase in the base level of relevant variable and the consequential burden for the public and private sectors.

In particular, infrastructure investment will be of public property regardless of whether it has been financed by the EU or national government funds. Public investment also includes the co-financing of investment in agriculture, fishery and industry, and is used in the model to determine the accumulation of the new public capital stock. In turn, private investment is increased by the private share of CSF intervention in hard and soft infrastructure and the EU and private finance part of CSF intervention in agriculture, fishery and industry.

We also model sectoral investment for the tradable, non-tradable and agricultural sectors, according to the diversification of the macroeconometric model outlined in the previous chapter. Tradable investment is augmented by the amount spent for actions in the industrial sector, while non-tradable investment embeds all investment flows regarding hard and soft infrastructure actions. Finally, agricultural investment is increased by the CSF amount spent for agriculture and fishery.

Public deficit increases by the amount of public co-financing of all sorts of investment and also by the public contribution to human capital training. Notice that private investment determines the evolution of total private capital stock that enters in the definition of public sector wealth in the consumption function.

Savings are reduced by the amount that the private sector has to contribute to the realisation of investment in agriculture, fishery and industry. However, the reduction of private savings is more than compensated by the increase in private investment flows.

The disposable income that enters the consumption function is augmented by the amount spent on training in the form of either remuneration to trainees or a fee to the trainers. In addition, we introduce two accumulation equations for hard and soft infrastructure to assess the improvement of the capital stocks relative to the base forecasting.

Table 4.2. Demand-side effects of CSF actions

Category	*Increment*
Public investment	*Public and EU finance part of CSF intervention in hard and soft infrastructure + Public finance part of CSF in agriculture, fishery and industry*
Private investment	*CSF finance in agriculture, fishery and industry* *+ Private finance part of CSF in hard and soft infrastructure*
Tradable investment	*CSF in industry*
Non-tradable investment	*CSF in hard and soft infrastructure*
Agricultural investment	*Total CSF finance in agriculture and fishery*
Public deficit	*Public finance of CSF in hard and soft infrastructure, agriculture, fishery, industry and training*
Wealth accumulation	*Private finance part of CSF in agriculture, fishery and industry*
Disposable income	*Total CSF finance in human capital training*

4. SUPPLY-SIDE EFFECTS

After having established in chapter 2 the positive impact of policies for a rise of public infrastructure on output, the next step is to calibrate some new parameters in the estimated model, in order to study economy-wide effects. In an econometric model, such as the one employed in this study, the effect of infrastructure and human capital improvement can be analysed by introducing a number of supply-side effects in the estimated equations for output and production costs.

4.1. Hard Infrastructure

The CSF effect is obtained by augmenting the simulated growth rate of sectoral output in the base simulation by the corresponding output elasticity with respect to hard infrastructure. A number of empirical studies offer diverging evidence on the impact of this type of infrastructure on output. Table 2.1 has summarised this evidence focusing on estimates from European countries and cross-section data from OECD economies; in most cases, the effects are statistically significant, but vary substantially across countries.

Given this range of values, we opted for a total effect of hard infrastructure on output in Greece that amounts to only 4.5%. This value is the lowest average estimate for major OECD economies, and is also very close to the lowest bound of output elasticities of public capital surveyed by Munnell (1992). Albeit it is significantly lower than the estimated elasticity of infrastructure for large-scale manufacturing in Greece (reported in Table 2.1), we opted for this conservative value to avoid the common criticism against some implausibly high values of elasticities.[15]

Given the correlation coefficients reported in chapter 2, we also assume that supply-side effects of infrastructure can differ across sectors. For instance, the tradable sector is assumed to be the readiest to incorporate the improvement of hard infrastructure into production, by means of energy savings, better transport, communication etc. The non-tradable, public and agricultural sectors also benefit from hard infrastructure but to a lesser extent, reflecting the lower capital intensity and the slower adaptation to new technologies. Therefore, elasticity values were chosen to be 1.5% for the tradable sector, and 1.0% for the non-tradable, public and agricultural sectors, respectively, summing up to a total impact of 4.5%.

4.2. Soft Infrastructure

Soft infrastructure actions will improve the social and cultural environment, enhance technological and educational capabilities, and bridge regional discrepancies by a multitude of local interventions. To capture these supply-side effects we assume that competition, measured by real unit labour cost (ratio of real wage rate to productivity) will improve.

The rise in soft infrastructure is expected to affect the real unit labour cost, first, through the impact on the real wage rate and, second, through the impact on productivity of the economy. The first effect results from the rise in the real value of the marginal product of labour, whilst the latter stems from the overall improvement in the productive environment of the economy. Given that projects in soft infrastructure involve a wide variety of actions in infrastructure formation (ranging from educational buildings and health spending to cultural activities) it is harder to quantify the overall effect on growth than in the case of hard infrastructure. Nevertheless, we assume that the effect on productivity leads to a gain in competition by outweighing the rise in real wages, and so the elasticity is set equal to -1%.[16]

To a considerable extent, actions of soft infrastructure also involve the public sector. Thus, we assume that public employment will increase above the level assumed in the base scenario. This implies that, albeit the number of persons employed in the public sector will not increase (in accordance to the Convergence Plan), *effective* public labour will rise as new technologies, monitoring, and evaluation schemes are introduced in the public sector. Absent any empirical studies on the magnitude of this type of effect, this elasticity is set equal to 5%. Given the estimated elasticities of public output with respect to public consumption and employment, the increase in public employment implies an automatic rise of public sector activity by approximately 1%. This value is similar to the effect of hard infrastructure, and, thus, there is no need to add another elasticity for output.

4.3. Productive Investment

This form of intervention involves mainly grants and subsidies that are expected to improve competitiveness and stimulate investment plans by the private sector. In the approach considered here, investment aid to manufacturing and agricultural sectors affects explicitly the capital stock and output in these sectors and, hence, there is no need to consider further supply-side effects stemming from such actions.

4.4. Education And Training

In a report of the European Business Confederation on the impact of CSF, Brennan (1993) assesses that for Greece, the most immediate and direct impact of CSF spending on competitiveness has been through the training programmes that have resulted in substantial productivity gains. The effect of human resources funding of training activities is measured by the extent it raises the employment of skilled workers. To assess the number of skilled workers that will be added to the labour force, we first assume that each trainee receives a fraction μ (set at 30%) of the wage rate in the non-tradable sector, while instructors are remunerated the full rate and each of them trains a group of people. The annual bill is then given by:

Annual CSF finance = μ(trained workers per year) + (trainees) * (wage rate in the non-tradable sector)*

The number of trained workers, which gives a measure of the investment in human capital for the country, is added to the stock of skilled workers according to an accumulation process similar to that of physical capital:

Skilled workers = (1-ε)(existing skilled workers) + (trained workers per year)*

The number of skilled workers depends on the depreciation rate ε. In his studies of EU structural policies, Pereira (1997, 1999) sets this rate equal to zero, as he assumes that aggregate public knowledge (e.g. secondary education) tends to be maintained at the society level.

However, given that the human capital stock is proxied here by the *number* of skilled workers, we opt for a positive rate of depreciation ε, to account for exit from skilled workforce (due e.g. to technological progress, retirement etc). This rate is set equal to 5% per annum, which is slightly higher than the depreciation rate of physical capital in Greece, as we assume that, due to physical capital irreversibility, firms are more likely to adopt technologies that render human, rather than physical, capital obsolete.

A data series for the number of skilled workers has been constructed by assuming that the skilled workforce consists of employees that are secondary education graduates. According to the latest available data for Greece, the fraction of high school graduates in total workforce is close to 50%, and so in the non-CSF simulations we assume that one half of existing employment is composed of skilled workers.[17]

Next, to model the aggregate effect brought about by the increase of skilled workforce, we assume that unit labour cost (competition) of the economy in real terms improves depending on the fraction of skilled workers in total workforce. The expected effect of the increase in skilled human resources is, first, the overall improvement of labour productivity. This effect is found to be significantly positive by cross section studies. For instance, Barro and Lee (1994) find that an additional year of secondary schooling raises the growth rate by an annual average of 1.3 percentage points for a sample of 116 countries, while Barro and Sala-I-Martin (1995) report similar findings. Existing empirical evidence on the effects of human capital on total output in Greece shows that its elasticity amounts to 0.26; this figure is close the average elasticity for the twenty highest economies which amounts to 0.23.[18]

On the other hand, as the proportion of skilled workers increases, we would expect a higher average wage rate in the economy, as the compensation of the -more productive- skilled workforce is higher than the corresponding one for unskilled workers. However, albeit the present expected value of a worker's remuneration should reflect his/her future productivity, the former rises significantly with age and so initial real wages may well be lower than productivity, particularly for younger (or newly hired) trained workers (see Kotlikoff and Gokhale, 1992).[19] Therefore, as in the case of soft infrastructure, the net effect of education financing on the growth rate of real unit labour cost, i.e. on the difference between the rise in the real wage rate and the rise in productivity, is set equal to -1%.

The supply-side effects of CSF intervention are summarised in Table 4.3, while the values of supply-side elasticities to the various types of CSF intervention by type of effect for each sector are summarised in Tables 4.4.a and 4.4.b.

Table 4.3. Supply-side effects of CSF actions

Category	*CSF intervention*
Growth rate of sectoral output	*Elasticity of sectoral output w. r. t. Hard infrastructure * (% rise in hard infrastructure)*
Growth rate of real unit labour cost	*Elasticity of real unit labour cost w. r. t. Soft infrastructure *(% rise in soft infrastructure)*
	*Elasticity of real unit labour cost w. r. t. skilled workers * (% rise in skilled workers)*
Public employment	*Elasticity of public employment w. r. t. Soft infrastructure * (% rise in soft infrastructure)*

Table 4.4.a. Imposed impact elasticities (θ) of key variables with respect to CSF actions

Type of effect	*Hard Infrastructure*	*Soft Infrastructure*	*Human Resources*
Tradable output	0.015		
Non-tradable output	0.01		
Public output	0.01		
Public employment		0.05	
Agricultural output	0.01		
Real unit labour cost		-0.01	-0.01

Table 4.4.b. Simulated average output elasticities with respect to hard infrastructure

Period	$\Delta S/S^B$	$\Delta Y/Y^B$	Average elasticity
1995 – 2001	15.1%	2.5%	0.17
2001 – 2010	16.5%	1.75%	0.11

Note: For the definition of the variables see Box 6.

Box 6: The hard infrastructure multiplier

In chapter 2 we presented a number of empirical studies attempting to estimate the elasticity (ε) of output (Y) with respect to a rise in infrastructure capital stock (S). In particular, a proportional increase in the latter will cause a rise in output given by:

$$\Delta Y/Y^B = \varepsilon * (\Delta S/S^B)$$

where Y^B and S^B denote a base level of output and infrastructure respectively, and ΔY, ΔS denote the deviation from those levels:

$$\Delta Y = Y - Y^B \text{ and } \Delta S = S - S^B$$

As shown in Table 2.1 the elasticity for manufacturing output in Greece is found to be 0.18 when a static production function is estimated. Practically, this means that a 10% rise in infrastructure capital will lead to a 1.8% increase in large-scale manufacturing output. However, the sectoral model has a dynamic structure and the effect of public capital on output is delineated into three phases:

(i) impact elasticity: This denotes the immediate effect that a rise in infrastructure has on output before triggering the multiplier effects in the model. Following the static models of chapter 2, we impose the impact effect as an additive term in the sectoral output equations:

$$(\Delta Y / Y^B{}_t) = (equation) + \theta * (\Delta S / S^B{}_t)$$

where θ is the impact elasticity of public capital (see Table 4.4.a).

(ii) annual elasticity: After solving the model within a period of time (i.e. a year in the present model), one obtains the total effect produced by the rise in infrastructure through the economy-wide interactions of demand and supply.

(iii) average elasticity: The dynamic structure of the model implies that the effects of a rise in public capital are propagated over time and in each period they conflate with the effects produced by further changes in infrastructure. After evaluating the ratio of average output growth to the average rise in hard infrastructure, we obtain the average elasticity.

The average elasticity yields a more representative estimate of the public capital effect on output, which is comparable to the findings of the static models presented in chapter 2. To ensure that the average elasticity of total output with respect to hard infrastructure is close to the conservative estimate of Table 2.1, we set the impact elasticities of the various components of output with respect to hard infrastructure as shown in the first column of Table 4.4.a. The simulated results are presented in Table 4.4.b. and appear to be slightly more conservative than the static estimates.

5. ASSESSING THE MACROECONOMIC IMPACT OF CSF

For each category of CSF intervention, the model is simulated in order to assess two types of macroeconomic impact depending on whether the supply-side effects described in the previous section are either absent or fully realised. In the first case, the simulation results could be considered as 'partial' as they depict only the demand effects of CSF actions. In the second case, results describe the 'full' impact of CSF stemming from both demand- and supply-side effects. A summary of the numerical results on growth and employment (at aggregate and sectoral level) is given in Table 4.5.

It should be noted that besides the distinction between demand and supply-side effects, another crucial assumption is made about the course of stabilisation policy. As already discussed, we assume that during the implementation of CSF the Convergence Plan continues unabated and achieves the same debt-to-output targets as projected in the base scenario. Employing a simple fiscal rule, according to which the direct tax rate is risen until a specified debt target is met in each period, ensures the achievement of the targets. Under this assumption, no direct change will occur in the debt burden or the public deficit as a consequence of CSF actions. The changes will appear now in the primary deficit that is upwards influenced by the co-financing obligations of CSF and downwards by the increased revenues generated by the higher tax base.

5.1. Hard Infrastructure

In the absence of supply-side effects, output rises by nearly 2% during the four-year implementation of CSF, but when the intervention expires output is hard-landed to base levels. This result shows that no permanent effect should be expected, unless the supply-side effects of physical infrastructure are realised. The growth rate of output initially rises, but then returns to baseline, and the same occurs for the growth rate of productivity. Employment rises in the period of CSF implementation but then falls below the base case, due to the higher wages that have been struck during the period of the boom and drive some people out of jobs.

The situation is different when supply-side effects are taken into account. Output will be found to be 2.4% above the baseline at the end of the simulation period, after growing at a rate higher by 0.1 percentage units per annum in average. New employment is generated and this type of intervention is expected to create around 80,000 new jobs. Despite the increase in employment, the output growth dominates and productivity grows at rate 0.1 percentage units per annum faster than in the base. The increase in output remains after the terminal period of the plan. This reveals that when supply-side externalities are present the effects of this type of intervention have a permanent character and do not evaporate after the ending of CSF.

5.2. Soft Infrastructure

In the case of soft infrastructure, output increases during the implementation period but then virtually returns to baserun level in the absence of supply-side effects. In average, output rises annually by approximately half relative to the case of hard infrastructure, both in the absence and the presence of supply-side effects. This reflects the fact that total soft interventions are considerably below the amount allocated to the hard ones. However, in the presence of supply-side effects the rise in output and labour productivity is stronger. This is due to the fact that soft infrastructure exerts a downward impact on the real cost of labour, which in turn lowers prices and increases competitiveness. Finally, it is noteworthy that tradable and agricultural output fall below baseline for soft infrastructure actions, as the latter are mainly oriented to the non-tradable and public sectors. This underlines the importance of interdependencies for the successful implementation of CSF, as the stabilisation rule imposed to ensure the achievement of budget surpluses via increased taxation exerts a downward pressure on sectoral potential of sectors that are not directly affected by CSF actions.

5.3. Aid To Production Investment

The increase in investment flows in the tradable and agricultural sectors boosts output and employment. The consequential rise of the corresponding capital stocks ensures that the positive impact remains strong for a long period after the end of CSF interventions, though output and productivity return to baseline growth rates. As all actions in agriculture are incorporated in this type of intervention, agricultural output displays the largest increase, compared to other types. It should be recalled that no supply-side effects are assumed for this intervention, since it directly extra passes on the production function.

5.4. Education And Training

In the absence of supply-side effects, the human resource programme degenerates to a pure income transfer to participants of purposeless training. This could lead to temporary increases in consumption and output, but the operation of the stabilisation rule ensures a one-to-one increase in taxation in order to achieve the debt targets. As a result, output increases only slightly relative to the baseline level, while the base growth rate remains unaffected after the terminal period of the Plan.

The situation is very different when supply-side effects are taken into account and real labour cost is brought down. A growth process is initiated and the boost in competitiveness increases activity, output and productivity grow at a higher pace than in the baseline, and real wages improve. This erodes part of the jobs that could have been created, particularly in the non-tradable sector where prices are dependent to a larger extent on domestic unit labour cost. As a result, employment in the non-tradable sector is only slightly higher than in the absence of supply-side effects.

5.5. Overall CSF Effects

The CSF will affect the economy through the cumulative impact of the separate actions. In the absence of supply-side effects, output will rise by 4.2% during the total period of CSF actions, but then will improve by only 2% over base level, mainly due to the impact of private productive investment. Growth rates of output and productivity fall below baseline after the end of CSF transfers and return to the base levels after some periods. The wage increases associated with the boom raise the participation rate, and at the same time some jobs will be created. However, unemployment may slightly rise after a period of containment during the implementation years of the CSF.

When all types of supply-side effects are taken into account, during the CSF implementation period output growth rate rises on average by 1.0% and employment expands by 140,000 new jobs over the base employment.[20] Also, total output in year 2005 will be higher than baseline by an impressive 5.2%. More importantly, output growth rate is above baseline rate by 0.1 percentage units, while annual productivity growth is 0.2% higher over the period of simulation.

Similar conclusions are reached by the implementation of the CSF simulation exercise in the HERMIN models for Ireland, Portugal and Spain (Bradley et al., 1995b). Although the exercise is different in nature,[21] the 'Keynesian' (demand) effects have short lasting effects on output while, on the other hand, the existence of supply-side effects produces a permanent positive impact on output growth.

It is to be noted here that our estimates somehow differ from official EU calculations, which underestimate the growth impact and overestimate the employment effect. According to these estimates '[between 1994 and 1999] in terms of average annual growth rates, this impact represents an additional growth rate of 0.9 percentage points. In the 1994-99 period, the employment supported by structural aid rises to 180,000 jobs' (European Commission, 1997a, p. 36). This growth difference can be explained by the more detailed accounting of supply-side effects in our modelling. The reason that despite higher growth our model predicts fewer employment gains can be explained by technological advancement which 'shades' some hiring opportunities, and also to the adoption of flexible labour demand and supply.[22]

Table 4.5. Effects of CSF on output and employment

Variable		Hard Infrastructure CSF	Hard Infrastructure Post-CSF	Soft Infrastructure CSF	Soft Infrastructure Post-CSF	Competitiveness CSF	Competitiveness Post-CSF	Human Resources CSF	Human Resources Post-CSF	Total CSF	Total Post-CSF
Output at factor cost	DE	1.5	-0.3	0.8	-0.1	2.0	2.1	0.3	0.5	4.2	2.1
	SE	2.5	1.7	1.2	0.6	-	-	0.4	1.0	5.8	5.4
Tradable sector output	DE	1.4	-2.0	0.8	-1.1	1.5	-0.6	0.3	0.3	3.7	-3.0
	SE	2.7	-0.2	1.1	-0.4	-		0.6	1.4	5.5	0.3
Non-tradable sector output	DE	2.2	0.1	1.2	0.1	1.9	1.1	0.4	0.8	5.3	1.9
	SE	3.5	2.7	1.5	0.5	-	-	0.4	1.1	6.8	5.2
Agricultural output	DE	-0.1	-0.5	0.0	-0.2	5.7	14.5	0.0	0.0	5.5	13.5
	SE	1.6	1.2	0.0	-0.2	-	-	0.0	0.1	7.2	15.4
Output growth rate	DE	0.1	-0.3	0.1	-0.2	0.4	-0.2	0.1	-0.0	0.6	-0.6
	SE	0.4	-0.2	0.2	-0.1	-	-	0.1	0.1	1.0	-0.5
Total employment	DE	42.8	-16.4	22.7	-8.5	37.3	9.0	7.6	16.2	101.3	0.0
	SE	66.3	38.9	38.3	10.4	-		8.9	26.4	141.7	82.0
Tradable sector employment	DE	10.1	-15.7	5.4	-8.1	9.7	-2.9	1.8	3.7	24.7	-21.7
	SE	16.9	-0.5	7.2	-4.2	-	-	3.0	11.4	34.4	3.6
Non-tradable sector employment	DE	32.7	-0.7	17.3	-0.4	27.6	11.9	5.7	12.5	76.6	21.7
	SE	49.4	39.4	20.1	0.7	-	-	6.0	15.0	96.4	64.8

Notes: The column 'CSF' displays the average effects over the second CSF implementation period (1995-2001), and column 'Post-CSF' displays the average effects over the post-CSF period (2002-2005). The row 'DE' displays simulation results with only demand-side effects, and row 'SE' the results when both demand- and supply-side effects are taken into account. Output is expressed as proportional change from base, and output growth rate and employment as absolute differences.

Box 7: An assessment of the actual impact of the CSF in Greece

Using the model, an attempt can be made to assess the impact of CSF actions with respect to the outcome of the non-intervention case. The estimate of the actual CSF impact for the period 1995-99 results from the difference between base projections (that do not take into account CSF) and actual outcomes.

In particular, output growth is estimated to be higher due to CSF by 0.4 and 0.5 percentage points for 1995 and 1996 respectively. Also, 52,000 additional jobs are created in 1995 while the corresponding figure for 1996 is 55,000 jobs. It appears that the first two years of the 1994-99 programme have only marginally contributed to the acceleration of the growth process. This fact may be attributed to the low absorption rates in the beginning of CSF. It is estimated that only 30% of total planned inflows for the period 1994-99 have been absorbed during the period 1994-96.[23]

The situation appears to be significantly improved for 1997, 1998 and 1999 when absorption rates increased significantly, exceeding 75% of total planned inflows. For these three years 1.9, 2.3 and 1.9 percentage points respectively of the achieved growth rate can be attributed to growth boosted by CSF, while the average annual increase of growth over the 1995-99 period is estimated to be 1.4 percentage points.

Regarding employment, only 32,000 additional new jobs respectively are due to CSF in 1997, as the actual outcome in employment was affected by external factors, such as low-wage migration flows from the Balkan and former Eastern economies. The situation ameliorates significantly during 1998 and 1999 when it is estimated that around 130,000 and 152,000 new jobs respectively are generated by growth boosted by the CSF, giving rise to an average of 84,000 new jobs annually over the 1995-99 period.

Figure 4.1. CSF impact on growth

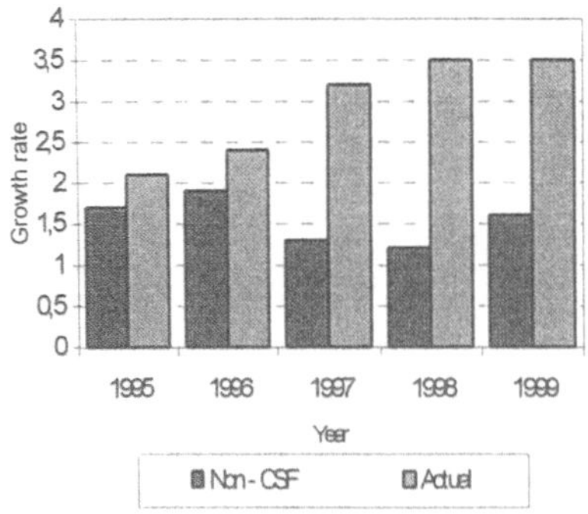

Figure 4.2. CSF impact on employment

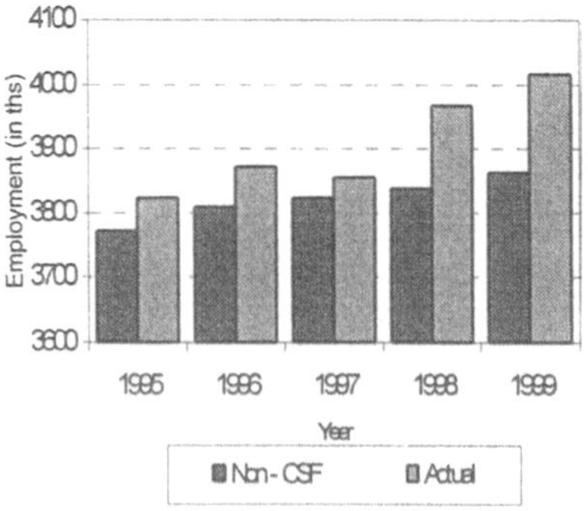

Chapter 5

ENERGY DEMAND AND THE ENVIRONMENTAL EFFECTS OF CSF

1. ENERGY DEMAND IN GREECE

In Greece the demand for energy is a substantial element in the analysis of both environmental effects and economic perspectives for the following reasons:

- energy is a crucial determinant of production costs. Thus, energy prices play a key role in assessing productivity trends of the various sectors.
- a substantial part of energy consumption in Greece is imported and so the pattern of future demand can be used to assess the course of trade balance and the energy dependence of the country.
- energy consumption in Greece is subject to various taxes. A scheme for energy taxation is discussed in order to reduce CO_2 emissions and improve environmental standards. Thus, energy forecasting can help to assess the expected impact of energy taxation on state revenues and the environment.

This chapter seeks to assess the future demand for energy in Greece by sector and by type, and investigate how this demand is affected by the implementation of the CSF. The forecasts are based on estimated demand equations for each sector of economic activity (traded, non-traded, public and agricultural sector) and for each type of energy (oil, electricity and solid fuels). The energy system is then integrated into the macroeconometric model, so that all interactions between energy, prices and production factors are properly taken into account.

The demand for energy in Greece is closely related to output growth and has followed similar patterns. Given that during the 1960's the Greek economy experienced one of the highest growth rates among OECD economies, energy consumption was increasing at fast rates, and averaged 12% per annum for the period 1960-1973. The rapid industrialisation process was accompanied by large energy needs: energy intensity in the industrial sector (defined as energy consumption relative to output) almost doubled during the period 1960-1973. Energy intensity in the other sectors of the economy was also increasing, albeit at slower rates.[24]

The two oil price shocks led to a fall in output growth and energy demand. This implies strong income elasticities of energy demand. As a result of slower output growth, the growth rate of energy consumption fell to an average annual rate of 5.6% for the period 1975-1980 and 2.3% during the decade after. Moreover, the industrial share of energy, after reaching 39.1% in 1980, started to decline and fell to 29% in 1990. In contrast, the transport sector has shown a rising trend -mostly triggered by the increasing demand for car fuels.

The largest part of energy consumption consists of oil and electricity (92% of total on 1994), while the rest is solid fuel (coal) consumed by the industrial sector and, more particularly, by the large-scale cement industry. Domestic energy sources consist mainly of coal and are a substantial part of total consumption. Domestic oil production is minimal and a large part of energy is still imported, though the degree of energy dependence is improving during the last decade.

The industrial sector has shown a growing demand for electricity, while the oil share has been diminished during the 1980's as industries were seeking alternative energy sources after the price increases. The solid fuel share does not show any noticeable change. The pattern of consumption in the commercial/residential sector has also been shifted towards electricity; the share of the latter increased from 20.2% in 1970 to 31.9% in 1980 and reached 36.2% in 1990. However, with an average growth rate of 1.3% over the 1980-90 period, it expanded at a slower pace than the average annual rate of 4.3% in International Energy Agency (IEA) countries. Finally, consumption by the transport sector -which uses mainly oil- has been constantly growing due to the ever-increasing number of vehicles in Greece.

Energy prices were falling in real terms until 1973, but then closely followed the rise in oil prices. The sharp oil price rises in 1974 and 1980 caused similar increases in electricity prices, since oil constitutes a substantial input for electricity production. The GDP deflator was growing with an average rate of 15.2% during 1974-1980 and 18.9% during 1981-1990, while the price of oil grew by 23.0% and 14.9% and the price of electricity by 17.8% and 17.1% for the corresponding periods. The currently heavy dependence of electricity generation on oil is expected to change in the future only with the introduction of natural gas.

To capture the effects of energy on the productive side of the economy, we consider first the demand for energy by each sector. The production bloc consists of three aggregate sectors: (a) the tradable sector that includes manufacturing and mining, (b) the non-tradable sector that includes transport and commercial activities and (c) the aggregation of public and agricultural sectors. The distinction is made in order to conform with the annual four-sector macroeconometric model for Greece (described in chapter 3) to which the present energy demand system is incorporated for forecasting and simulation analysis.

Since data published for the commercial, residential and transport sectors include energy used aggregately by the non-tradable and the public and agricultural sectors taken together, demand for energy in each of those categories is obtained proportionally to the output share of those sectors:

Energy demand by non-tradable sector =
(Total energy demand - Energy demand by tradable sector)(Non-tradable sector output/Total output - Tradable sector output)*

Energy demand by public and agricultural sectors =
(Total energy demand) – (Energy demand by tradable and non-tradable sectors)

Finally, the demand for solid fuel (that amounts to around 5% of total energy) is not modelled behaviourally but serves as a residual between total energy demanded by the three sectors and the demand for the two previously estimated types of energy. The residual equation is:

Demand for solid fuel = (Total energy demand) – (Demand for oil and electricity)

A description of the type of demanded energy by sector is given in Table 5.1.

Table 5.1. Demand for energy types by sector

Sectors *Types*	*Industry*	*Transport*	*Residential and Commercial*
1. Solid	Solid fuels	-	-
2. Liquid	Oil, Fuel oil	Gasoline, Fuel Oil, Diesel Oil	Oil
3. Electricity	Electricity	Electricity	Electricity

Box 8: Types of energy demand

Quantities of energy consumed by *sector* are divided in the following three categories in accordance with the classification in the Annual Energy Balances, issued by the Ministry for Development:

1. Industry: Consumption by the extractive industries, manufacturing and construction.

2. Transportation: Consumption for transportation irrespective of transport means, excluding consumption for international sea transport and including energy consumption for all air-transport activities.

3. Housing/Commercial: Consumption of households, commercial establishments, services, agriculture etc.

Quantities by *type* of energy are divided in the following three categories in accordance with the classification in the Annual Energy Balances, issued by the Ministry for Development :

a. Solid fuel: Brown coal (lignite), brown coal briquettes, hard coal (calorific value higher than 5,700 Kcal/kg) and coke-oven coke.

b. Oil: Gasoline, aviation fuels, diesel, fuel oil, LPG, kerosene, naphtha, petroleum coke and refinery gas.

c. Electricity: Production by the Greek Public Power Corporation and self-production at the firm level.

Demand for energy by type is made through the three main sectors of economic activity for the period 1974-1994: the industrial sector, the transport sector and the residential-commercial sector. Using this classification, the various types of energy are grouped in three categories:

(i) Solid fuels that include all solid sources of energy consumed by industry

(ii) Liquid fuels including petrol consumed by industry, gasoline, diesel and fuel oil consumed by the transport sector and heating-oil used by the housing and commercial sectors

(iii)Electricity consumed by all three sectors.

The energy demand in each production sector is a function of sectoral output and the real price of energy in each sector, where:

(i) the real price of energy in the tradable sector is the ratio of energy price in industry to the tradable sector output deflator

(ii) the real price of energy in the non-tradable and public-agricultural sectors is defined as the ratio of an expenditure-weighted price index of energy in the transport, housing and commercial sectors, to non-tradable sector output deflator.

The econometric methodology outlined in chapter 3 was also followed in this case and a full listing of the model equations and identities is given in the Appendix.

The equations for sectoral demand of energy have been estimated and the main results are shown in Table 5.2. The long-run output elasticities are 0.76, 1.51 and 1.95 for the tradable, non-tradable and public-agricultural sectors respectively, while the corresponding short-run elasticities are 0.79, 1.27 and 0.64.

Regarding the price elasticities, they are found to be -0.19 and -0.24 in the long run for the tradable and non-tradable sectors respectively, while in the short-run they are found to be -0.25 and -0.23 respectively. The demand for energy by the public-agricultural sector appears to be insensitive to changes in real prices, probably because of the lower substitution possibilities with other production factors in these sectors of economic activity.

Demand equations for the various types of energy are modelled as functions of the associated price indices relative to GDP deflator by using total output as a measure of activity. Own-price coefficients are expected to be negative. Positive activity coefficients indicate a 'luxury' type of energy that rises with output, while negative ones characterise a 'necessity' type of energy.

Table 5.2. Demand elasticities of energy with respect to output and prices

	Output		Price	
Energy demand	Long-run	Short-run	Long-run	Short-run
Tradable sector	0.76	0.79	-0.19	-0.25
Non-tradable sector	1.51	1.27	-0.24	-0.23
Public-agricultural sectors	1.95	0.64	-	-
Oil	1.00	0.78	-0.22	-0.16
Electricity	1.76	1.12	-	-0.14

Notes: Elasticities of sectoral energy demand are calculated with respect to sectoral output and sectoral real prices. Elasticities of demand for each type of energy are calculated with respect to total output and aggregate real prices.

The demand for oil has an output elasticity of 1.0 in the long-run, while the demand for electricity has a long-run output elasticity of 1.76. The short-run output elasticities are smaller (0.78 and 1.12 respectively). The own-price elasticities for oil is rather small (-0.22 and -0.16 in the long- and short-run respectively). The own-price elasticity for electricity is -0.14 in the short-run; the long-run elasticity is found statistically insignificant and is omitted from the long-run equation. Finally, the demand for electricity adjusts slower to its long-run equilibrium relationship (the adjustment parameter is -0.23 while that of oil demand is -0.51).

Energy prices are modelled with homogeneity of degree one imposed and accepted by the data. The domestic prices of energy components are modelled as functions of the domestic unit labour cost and the price of imported oil, which is equal to the price of crude oil in USD/barrel[25] multiplied by the Drachma/USD exchange rate. To account for the effect of taxes on domestic oil prices, the latter are adjusted by the average Value Added Tax rate.[26]

The results show the serious dependence of domestic oil prices on the external component; the price of oil is found to depend by 40% on the foreign price of oil while the latter explains only a small fraction of the electricity price (4%).[27] The aggregate price indices used for energy demand in the tradable and non-tradable sectors are modelled as convex weighted averages of the corresponding prices of the three types.

Finally, we model the effects of energy prices on the price mechanism of the annual macroeconometric model. The basic price equations in the macro model are modified so as to include an energy price composite index together with unit labour cost and the price of imports.[28] The composite price index is calculated as the sum of the products of the weights in final demand of each type of energy and the corresponding price. These three prices drive the remaining prices in the model.

The results suggest that the wholesale price index depends by 55% on domestic unit labour cost and by 18% on the price of imports, while the remaining 27% is due to the price of energy. The corresponding energy burden for the tradable and non-tradable output deflators is only 13% and 16% respectively.

The system is interacting with a number of macroeconomic variables that are determined in the four-sector econometric model. The linkages operate mainly through two channels. First, through sectoral output, which affects the demand for energy in each sector, and total output which affects the type of energy demand. Second, through the price mechanism, which is affected by energy prices and, in turn, transmits the change in prices in the economy through sectoral deflators and the wholesale price index (see Figure 5.1).

Figure 5.1. Linkages between the energy system and the macroeconometric model

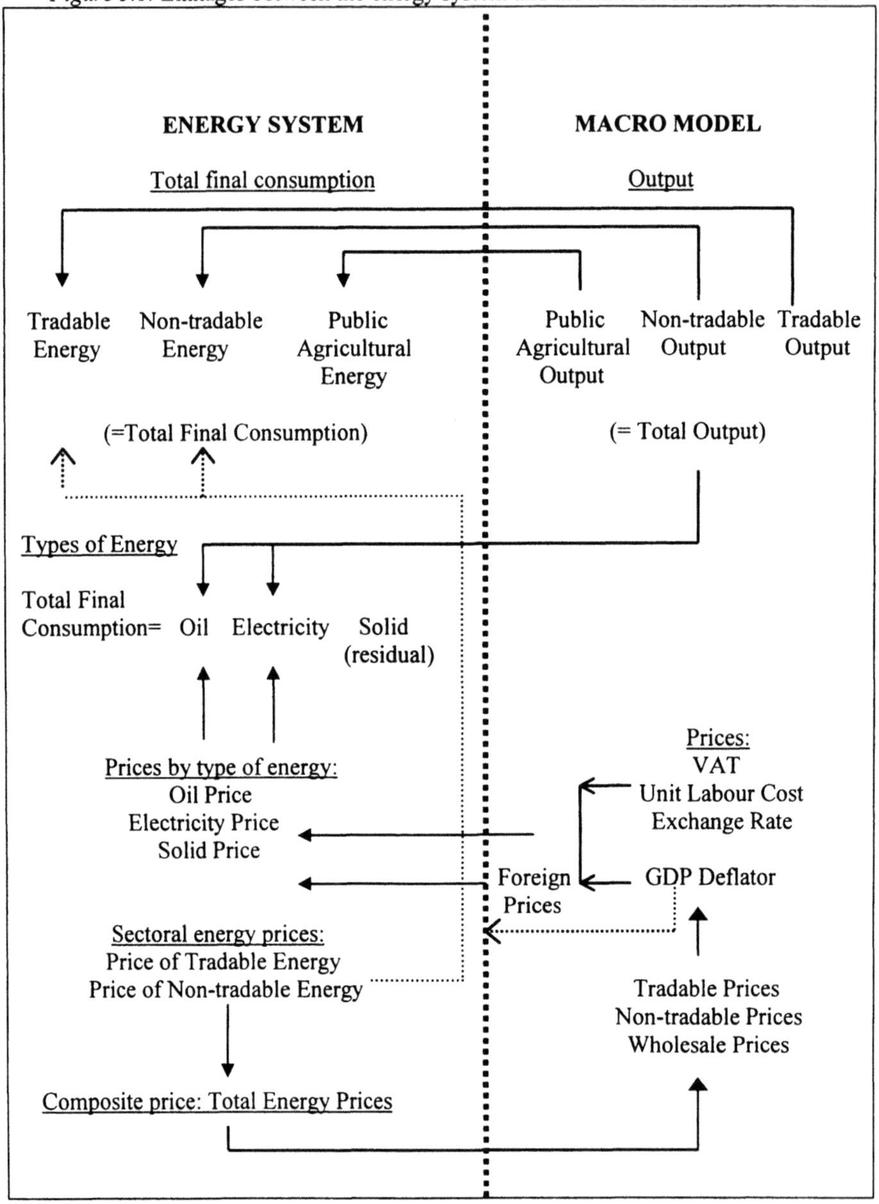

2. FORECASTS OF ENERGY DEMAND

To obtain the base forecast, the same assumptions as in chapter 3 were adopted with no other constant adjustment of endogenous variables to bring them closer to externally discernible values. For the two exogenous variables of the model, the international price of oil and the price of solid fuel the following two assumptions were adopted: (i) the international price of oil is assumed to remain constant, and (ii) the price of solid fuel is assumed to continue to grow at the same average rate that prevailed for the estimation period. The base solution is again obtained through a dynamic simulation of the model over the period 1995-2005, keeping single-equation errors at zero levels. The model is found to converge quickly to solution values, and to generate a reasonable base outcome for the energy variables.

The forecasts of the model compare well with actual annual energy consumption provided by the Ministry for Development for the years 1995 and 1996 (see Table 5.3). As expected, the base scenario underestimates total energy demand, while the absolute discrepancy[29] in the CSF scenario (which incorporates the cumulative effects of CSF actions) does not exceed 0.3%.

Table 5.3. Comparison between actual fuel consumption and model forecasts (in Mtoe) for years 1995 and 1996

	Oil	Electricity	Total
		1995	
Actual	10.8	2.9	14.7
Base	10.8 (0.6%)	2.9 (0.0%)	14.7 (-0.4%)
CSF	11.0 (2.2%)	3.0 (2.2%)	14.6 (-0.3%)
		1996	
Actual	11.6	3.1	15.6
Base	11.1 (-4.0%)	3.0 (-1.9%)	15.3 (-1.9%)
CSF	11.3 (-2.5%)	3.1 (2.1%)	15.6 (0.3%)

Note: Numbers in brackets are percent deviations from actual consumption.

Table 5.4 displays the model forecasts in terms of energy demand up to the year 2005. In absolute terms, total final energy demand will reach 20.1 Mtoe at year 2005, while the average annual growth rate for the period 1995-2005 is 3.1% p.a. The demand for energy in the tradable sector increases by an average 4.4% p.a., while the corresponding energy demand by the non-tradable sector increases by 3.5% p.a. The higher energy needs in the non-tradable sector in the base scenario reflect faster growth of non-tradable output relative to tradable sector output. During the same time period, the demand by the public-agricultural sector will increase by 1.3% p.a.

Table 5.4. Base forecasts of energy variables (in Mtoe) 1995-2005

Variable	**1995**	Average **1996-2000**	Average **2001-2005**
Total final consumption	14.6	16.4	19.0
Tradable sector	4.1	4.8	5.6
Non-tradable sector	6.1	6.8	8.5
Public-agricultural sector	4.4	4.8	4.9
Oil	10.8	11.7	13.4
Electricity	2.9	3.2	3.8

Turning to the demand for each energy type we observe that oil needs decrease over time relative to the demand for electricity; the former increase by 2.7% p.a. on average, thus reaching 70.4% of total final consumption at year 2005, while electricity demand increases by 3.3% p.a. and reaches 20.4% of total final consumption in 2005. The relative contributions of these two fuels for the year 1990 were 74.1% and 17.9% for oil and electricity respectively, resulting in a fall of the proportion of oil to electricity consumption from 4.1 in 1990 to 3.5 in 2005.

3. ENERGY-TAX SIMULATIONS

Using the model we can also consider the effects of a rise in energy prices on the demand for sectoral energy, the various types of energy and the GDP components. To examine the effects of a rise in energy prices in Greece brought about by an energy tax in the context of the present model, the price levels of oil and electricity were separately shocked by 10% (recall that the price of solid fuel is not modelled behaviorally and the demand for solid fuel is determined residually). In each simulation the rate of direct taxation to output was increased by 1 percentage point - which is roughly equiproportional to the expected rise of indirect tax revenues relative to output due to the energy tax- leaving the primary budget targets used in the base forecast unaffected.

A 10% rise in the price of oil reduces output by 0.1%, mainly as a result of the fall in tradable sector output (-0.4%). The fall in energy demand by the non-tradable sector is larger (-1.3%) relative to the tradable sector (-0.6%) at the terminal period 2005 while the demand by the public-agricultural sectors remains virtually unaffected due to the inelastic sectoral energy demand with respect to the relative price of energy. As expected, the reduction in the demand for oil is large (-1.7%) while electricity demand is also reduced (-0.2%) due to the fall in output.

A rise in the price of electricity by 10% produces a similar picture as in the case of the oil price shock -albeit of smaller proportions. A key difference involves the larger fall of energy demand by the tradable sector (-1.3) relative to the non-tradable sector (-0.9%) because the sectoral price index in the tradable sector is more heavily dependent on the price of electricity. Interestingly enough, the demand for electricity and oil remains unaffected in the long-run as it is found to be inelastic with respect to their own prices.

4. THE EFFECTS OF CSF ON ENERGY DEMAND

To assess the effect that the second CSF is going to have on energy demand in Greece we repeat the CSF modelling and analysis performed in chapter 4. The supply-side effects stem from the positive impact that improved infrastructure, more intensive capital formation and an upgraded labour force is expected to have on productivity growth. Part of these effects is due to CSF interventions involving the energy sector per se through a number of projects such as:

Box 9: The energy tax

Based on the 1990 EU commitment through the Council of the Community's Energy and Environment Ministers to stabilise CO_2 emissions by the year 2000 at the 1990 level, several studies have attempted to investigate the effects of an energy tax on energy consumption. This type of tax -imposed on all energy products in proportionality to their consumption- has two effects. First, it reduces energy consumption through the rise in prices and, second, it increases the general energy price index, thus generating inflationary pressures which result in a loss of competitiveness and a fall in economic activity; the latter effects induces a further fall in energy consumption through output elasticities.[30]

Standaert (1992) reports that a 10 USD per barrel tax will reduce GDP growth by 0.1 percentage points and raise the price level by 3.5% in year 2005 in the four major European economies (Germany, France, Italy and U.K). Karadeloglou (1992) considers the effects of the same energy tax in these countries and finds that the energy reduction will be relatively larger in the industrial sector due to the larger sectoral demand elasticities with respect to prices.

At this stage an important remark should be made regarding the nature of these experiments: as an energy tax results in a rise of tax revenues it also affects -directly or indirectly- disposable income of households through income taxation. Therefore, the assumption of budget neutrality is often adopted by decreasing the rate of taxation so as to keep the effects on the primary surplus (deficit) at the base level.

Under this assumption, an energy tax may even have a positive impact on output, if it alleviates other forms of distortionary taxation. Patsouratis and Souflis (1995) survey the evidence on European countries and report that a reduction of CO_2 emissions by one third through an energy tax will result in a fall of the GDP growth rate by around 0.1 to 0.5 percentage units in the case of budget neutrality, regardless of whether energy taxation triggers a fall in direct income taxation, social security contributions or indirect taxation.

(i) The construction of the natural gas distribution system, including the backbone pipeline from Russia and the installation for transferring liquid gas from Algeria.

(ii) Projects related to energy production and energy saving, including the development of efficient production methods from renewable energy sources (RES), the improvement of conventional thermal generation techniques based on lignite, and the installation of emission-reducing equipment.

In particular, the objectives of these projects aim at:

- Reducing the dependence on a single energy type or a specific production plant. This will improve efficiency of production, increase availability of alternative energy sources and eliminate shortages.
- Improving environmental standards, by reducing CO_2 emissions and increasing the rational use of more environment-friendly resources.

Certainly, each of those objectives is expected to have a positive impact on production. However, in the present context the supply-side effects are not modelled particularly for the energy sector, but aggregately for the four types of total CSF interventions as considered earlier. The positive effects brought about by the energy projects are assumed to be part of the effects generated by the combination of hard infrastructure, soft infrastructure, the rise in productive investment and the upgrading of human resources.

The calibration and treatment of the aggregate supply-side effects were described in detail in chapter 4. Table 5.5 shows the developments for energy in the two scenaria, namely without and with supply-side effects. In the first case, total demand for energy rises over the CSF intervention years (1.6% in 1996, 3.9% in 1998 and 6.1% in 2000) but falls after the intervention is over. The average growth rate of total final consumption over the period 1995-2005 is only 0.5% above baseline and at the end of the forecasting period the demand for energy will be higher by 5.0% than in the baseline scenario. In average, the demand for oil exceeds the base level by 3.4% while the corresponding rise for electricity will be higher by 5.5%. The rise in demand is mainly fuelled by the increased needs of the non-tradable sector, while tradable sector demand for energy virtually returns to baseline.

However, the picture changes starkly when supply-side effects are taken into account. Total energy consumption is higher by 5.0% for the CSF and by 10.2% for the post-CSF periods compared to the base level, while the annual average growth rate of energy demand for the period 1995-2005 is above baseline by approximately 0.9 percentage units amounting to an average of 6.9% p.a.. The demand for oil will be higher by 7.5%, and the demand for electricity by 11.3% in post-CSF period. On average, demand for electricity is higher by 8.8% p.a. for the period 1995-2005 while the demand for oil increases by 5.1% p.a., compared to the base scenario; thus CSF intervention causes a rise in the relative share of the demand for electricity. Finally, the corresponding energy needs of the tradable sector and non-tradable sectors increase on average by 3.3% and 12.1% respectively relative to baseline after the CSF.

Table 5.5. CSF effects on energy demand

Variable		CSF	Post-CSF
Total energy consumption	DE	3.7	5.9
	SE	5.0	10.2
Growth rate of total energy consumption	DE	1.0	-0.4
	SE	1.4	0.1
Demand by tradable sector	DE	2.4	0.3
	SE	3.3	3.3
Demand by non-tradable sector	DE	5.6	7.4
	SE	6.9	12.1
Demand by public-agricultural sectors	DE	2.2	9.8
	SE	3.9	15.1
Demand for oil	DE	2.8	4.5
	SE	3.8	7.5
Demand for electricity	DE	5.3	5.9
	SE	7.3	11.3
Energy price index inflation	DE	1.5	0.4
	SE	1.5	1.2

Notes: All variables are percent deviations from baseline except of the growth rate of total final consumption and the energy price inflation rate which are in absolute differences from baseline. The row 'DE' displays simulation results without supply-side effects, and row 'SE' the results with supply-side effects.

5. ENVIRONMENTAL EFFECTS OF CSF [31]

The developments in energy demand are closely linked to the environmental consequences of increased energy consumption. In the EU, negotiations amongst member states on the reduction of emissions started in 1990 and were finalised in June 1998 (see next box). The burden sharing agreement specifies that Greece will have to restrict the average growth of the emissions of all 6 gases for 2008-2012, to +25% compared to 1990 levels. This level will be achieved through a number of interventions (national and EU, common and co-ordinated policies and measures) in all sectors of the economy, and particularly in the energy sector.

Therefore, based on our forecasts of energy demand we derive projected CO_2 emissions for the extended period up to 2012, which is the terminal year of the internationally agreed period 2008-2012 for environmental action. In particular, attention is focused on the changes in CO_2 emissions brought about by the CSF. One of the major CSF interventions in Greece is the introduction of natural gas (NG) to the Greek energy system. The actual cost for the NG penetration is estimated at 2 billion Euro and is largely financed by the European Investment Bank. According to the works programme of Public Gas Corporation (PGC), total absorption of NG will reach 3.5 billion Nm^3 per year by 2005.[32] An extended infrastructure system has been designed and is now near completion in order to carry imported NG to the main consumption areas: first, in the electricity generation sector and large industrial units and, next, in the residential and commercial sectors -though at slower rates.[33]

In general, CO_2 emissions from the energy sector are directly related to fuel mix, combustion efficiency and technologies applied. In Greece, energy related activities (including extraction, distribution and combustion of fossil fuels) are responsible for approximately 76% of total national greenhouse gases emitted each year. During 1990-1995, CO_2 emissions from the energy sector accounted for approximately 90% of total CO_2 emissions in Greece, thus making this gas the largest contributor to the so-called 'greenhouse' effect.

Box 10: International agreements for the reduction of CO_2 emissions

Evidence of anthropogenic influence on climate, resulting in the international treaties signed in Toronto (1988), Rio de Janeiro (1992) and Kyoto (1997) for controlling atmospheric gases, shows that economic growth and energy consumption are also closely related to environmental considerations. Special attention is starting to be paid to the decrease of carbon dioxide (CO_2) and other 'greenhouse' gas emissions that primarily arise from the consumption of energy.

The Council of Ministers of the European Union decided in October 1990 that CO_2 emissions should be stabilised by 2000 at the level of 1990. The decision was prompted among others, by the following factors (see Surrey, 1992): (a) the consequent action of other policy measures (e.g. traffic jams), which are related to the energy consumption and which have to in any case be enforced ('no regrets' policy), (b) the wide differences among interested countries, which call for common policy measures, (c) the necessity of switching to a more efficient use of energy sources, given the inability of substitution with other less pollutive ones and (d) the importance of developing a european know-how in this sector.

Convinced of the necessity of further action on this matter, the world community adopted, in December 1997, the Kyoto Protocol to the United Nations Framework Convention on Climate Change (UNFCCC). The Kyoto Protocol sets out further commitments of the developed country Parties of the UNFCCC for the period 2008-2012. The overall target agreed is a reduction of the aggregate anthropogenic emissions of carbon dioxide (CO_2), methane (CH_4), nitrous oxide (N_2O), hydrofluorocarbons (HFCs), perfluorocarbons (PFCs) and sulphur hexafluoride (SF_6) by at least 5% below the 1990 levels for the period 2008-2012. The Protocol has also set out a differentiated approach for the achievement of the reduction target among the Parties involved. Under the provisions of Article 4 that enables the joint fulfilment of the commitments undertaken, the overall target for the EU (-8%) will be achieved by an equitable burden sharing between EU member states. The burden sharing should take into account differences in the starting point, national circumstances and historic responsibility of each member state in the occurrence of the 'greenhouse' effect. Negotiations amongst EU member states were finalised during the Environment Council in June 1998.

For the period 1995-2012, CO_2 emissions are calculated by using weighted emission factors for oil, coal and NG disaggregated to the three economic sectors. The emission factors used correspond to aggregate values for the year 1995 and are summarised in Table 5.6.[34]

Table 5.6. Emission factors (in kt CO_2/ktoe) for Oil, Coal and NG

Fuel type	Tradable	Non-tradable	Public-Agricultural
Oil	3.17	2.74	3.17
Coal	4.20	n.a.	n.a.
NG	2.00	n.a.	2.00

Notes: n.a. denotes not available or not applicable.

In Greece, electricity is predominantly produced by the combustion of brown coal (lignite), heavy fuel oil and diesel oil. Smaller amounts are also produced from RES which involve mostly hydropower and wind power installations and account for approximately 5% of total electricity production. The calculation of emissions from the use of electricity takes into account the losses incurred during the transformation process at power plants brought about by changes in the average thermal efficiency over the period 1995-2012. The 'future anticipated' average thermal efficiency is estimated by considering the fuel mix for alternative scenarios. Total CO_2 emissions from the electricity production sector are calculated by applying appropriate emission factors for the different fuels used. These factors derive from the approved Intergovernmental Panel on Climate Change (IPCC) methodology for the completion of inventories of national greenhouse gases (see *National Inventory of Greenhouse and Other Gases for the period 1990-1995*).

The forecasting takes place under alternative assumptions about the environmental effects that CSF is likely to have on the Greek economy. First, a benchmark forecast presenting energy and environmental developments in the absence of CSF interventions and NG penetration in the energy system is examined. We then focus on environmental scenarios that incorporate the two main features of interest: the group of actions and initiatives incorporated and co-financed by CSF and the pivotal role of the introduction of NG in the energy sector. Thus, besides the *Benchmark* scenario, which reflects the absence of any new initiatives of any kind (and in that respect cannot be considered to be a business-as-usual scenario), three other scenarios are considered that differ from the benchmark by incorporating the planned use of NG and the CSF effects first separately (*Benchmark with NG* and *CSF* respectively) and then jointly (*CSF with NG*). In the *Benchmark with NG* scenario additional electricity demand is satisfied by the introduction of *NG*, while in the other two scenarios the impact of CSF on energy consumption and CO_2 emissions without and with *NG* penetration is examined.

Scenario I: Benchmark

The increase in electricity demand is primarily satisfied by the introduction of new lignite and steam coal power units in the interconnected (mainland) electricity distribution network. At the same time, electric utilities also invest in the area of RES, which are incorporated in the production system of islands to meet increasing power demand in the domestic and tertiary sector. The relative contribution of these systems to total electricity production increases in 2012 to about 10.2%. The installation of new, more efficient thermal units and additional interventions in older units (maintenance, combustion efficiency improvements) will result in an increase of the average overall thermal efficiency from 34% in 1995 to 36% in the period 2000-2012.

Scenario II: Benchmark with NG

The main difference from the previous scenario is the substitution of new lignite and steam coal units by NG units. It is assumed that, after 2000, additional electricity demand will be solely satisfied by the introduction of new gas-fired stations in the interconnected distribution network. The effect of the NG penetration to the average thermal efficiency for the period 2000-2012 is an increase to about 37%. At the same time, increased emphasis on RES penetration brings their relative contribution to 10.7%.

Scenario III: CSF

This scenario conforms with the demand *and* supply-side effects analysis developed in chapter 4. Here the increase in electricity demand is satisfied by the introduction of new gas, lignite and steam coal power units in the interconnected (mainland) electricity distribution network. The relative contribution of RES systems to total electricity production increases in 2012 to about 10%. The average overall thermal efficiency from 34% in 1995 increases to 38% in the period 2000-2012.

Scenario IV: CSF with NG

Similarly to *Benchmark with NG* scenario, after 2000 under the *CSF with NG* scenario, all additional electricity demand is solely satisfied by the introduction of new gas-fired stations in the interconnected distribution network, which absorb approximately 3.3 bm^3 by the year

2012. The average thermal efficiency for the target period increases to approximately 39% and the contribution of RES reaches about 10%. In addition, there is also a partial substitution of liquid fuels with NG in the tradable and public-tertiary sectors. The gradual penetration of NG into these sectors results in a final consumption of 860 ktoe, or equivalently 1 bm^3 of NG by the year 2012. Although this figure is smaller than the one expected by the PGC for the same period (PNGC, 1997), it is estimated that the penetration of NG into the domestic and tertiary sector will be rather slow due to inertia in the consumption of households and increased demand needs of gas by the electricity production sector (3.3 billion m^3 compared to 1.5 billion m^3, which also incorporates investment in CHP units by the industry sector).

6. FORECASTS OF CO_2 EMISSIONS UNDER ALTERNATIVE SCENARIOS

Using the *Benchmark* scenario forecasts for demand of oil, electricity and coal of Table 6.4, and the corresponding emission factors reported in Table 6.7, CO_2 emissions for the period 1995-2012 are calculated and presented in Table 6.8. For the period 1990-2012, CO_2 emissions are found to increase by an average annual growth rate of about 2.2%, thus amounting to an average of 117.1 Mt (or an average increase of 53%) for the 5-year target period 2008-2012 compared to the 1990 levels. During the target period 2008-2012, the bulk of these emissions is attributed to electricity production (53%), while contributions of the other sectors amount to 15% for the tradable sector, 21% for the non-tradable sector and 11% for the public and tertiary sectors. In absolute values, the ratio of CO_2 emissions to GDP (in 1970 prices) remains relatively constant compared to CO_2 emissions per capita for the same time period. By 2012, the former indicator increases by about 7% (or at an average annual growth rate of 0.3%), whilst the latter follows closely the increase rate of total CO_2 emissions, mainly due to the modest projected population growth rate (estimated at 6.5% from 1990 to 2012).

As displayed in the second part of Table 6.8 (*Benchmark with NG* scenario), the introduction of NG in electricity production sector has a marked effect on total CO_2 emissions in Greece. This can be attributed to both the lower carbon content of gas (0.6tC/Mtoe compared to indicative values of 1.4tC/Mtoe for lignite and 0.8tC/Mtoe for oil) and the improved overall thermal efficiency of electricity production stations. For the target period, average annual total CO_2 emissions amount to 108.8 Mt, or 42% above 1990 levels, compared to 53% for the *Benchmark* scenario. This increase results in an annual growth rate of approximately 1.8% that is slightly lower than that of GDP (1.9%) during the 1990-2012 period. Thus, it is not surprising to observe a reduction in the CO_2/GDP indicator, which stabilises to approximately 0.155 tCO_2/GDP compared to 0.158 tCO_2/GDP in 1990.

Results change considerably when the effects of CSF actions are included (*CSF* and *CSF with NG* scenarios). The results are presented in Table 5.7. Up to year 2000, CO_2 emissions are expected to increase almost linearly at an average annual growth rate of about 2.3%. After 2000 however, there is a marked reduction of the growth rate of CO_2 emissions to 1.9% p.a., brought about by increased replacement of coal by gas, especially for the case of *CSF with NG* scenario. Increased use of natural gas assumed by this scenario results in a more rapid decrease of average CO_2 emissions for the target period, which are less than those of the *Benchmark* and *CSF* cases, amounting to 114.4 Mt, or 50% higher compared to 1990 levels. Despite this rapid growth of emissions, the CO_2/GDP indicator stabilises at about 0.160t CO_2/GDP, and is about 1% higher than its 1990 value as rigorous changes in economic infrastructure lead to a GDP rise of approximately 48% compared to the 1990 levels. As expected, however, this is not the case for the CO_2/capita index that follows the increase of total CO_2 emissions in a manner similar to that of the *Benchmark* case.

It is also worth noting that Anton et al. (1999) derived similar results regarding the environmental effects of CSF in Spain. These authors found that a significant increase in CO_2 emissions should be expected, although they did not take into account changes in energy consumption structure and emission factors. Such changes may have a positive impact stemming from more extensive and effective usage of types of energy that are friendlier to the environment.

The model forecasts show that demand for energy rises faster in the non-tradable sector and, as a result, the share of energy consumption by the traded sector will be reduced. Also, the demand for oil increases slower than the demand for electricity and other fuels and the ratio of oil to electricity consumption will fall. In turn, the average annual growth rates of predicted CO_2 emissions under different scenarios are higher than world forecasts: Holtz-Eakin and Selden (1995) predict that CO_2 emissions will globally increase by the year 2025 with an average annual rate of 1.8%. As regards the European Union, estimations indicate an annual average increase of 1.1.% for the period 1995-2000, which will come down to 0.5% for the period 2001-2010 (European Commission, 1996).

Table 5.7. Forecasts of CO_2 emissions (in Mt) under alternative scenarios

Variable	**1995**	**2000**	**2005**	**Average 2008-2012**	**% change/year 1990-2012**
			Benchmark		
Total CO_2	81.6	91.5	103.2	*117.1*	*2.2%*
CO_2/GDP	0.157	0.160	0.163	*0.167*	*0.3%*
CO_2/capita	7.8	8.7	9.7	*10.9*	*1.9%*
			Benchmark plus NG		
Total CO_2	81.6	90.4	98.9	*108.8*	*1.8%*
CO_2/GDP	0.157	0.158	0.156	*0.155*	*-0.1%*
CO_2/capita	7.8	8.6	9.3	*10.1*	*1.5%*
			CSF		
Total CO_2	81.6 (0.0)	96.8 (5.8)	104.5 (1.3)	*117.1* *(0.0)*	*2.2%*
CO_2/GDP	0.154 (-2.1)	0.166 (3.6)	0.162 (-0.8)	*0.163* *(-2.1)*	*0.2%*
CO_2/capita	7.8 (0.0)	9.2 (5.8)	9.8 (1.3)	*10.9* *(0.0)*	*1.9%*
			CSF plus NG		
Total CO_2	81.6 (0.0)	95.9 (4.8)	103.5 (0.2)	*114.4* *(-2.3)*	*2.1%*
CO_2/GDP	0.154 (-2.1)	0.164 (2.6)	0.160 (-1.8)	*0.160* *(-4.3)*	*0.1%*
CO_2/capita	7.8 (0.0)	9.1 (4.8)	9.7 (0.2)	*10.7* *(-2.3)*	*1.8%*

Notes: The CO_2/GDP indicator is in units of t CO_2/1970 thousand DRS and the CO_2/capita indicator is in units of t CO_2/inhabitant. Numbers in brackets are % deviations from the 'Benchmark' scenario.

However, it should be stressed that the results, and particularly those obtained for the *CSF* and *CSF with NG* scenarios, are obtained by

However, it should be stressed that the results, and particularly those obtained for the *CSF* and *CSF with NG* scenarios, are obtained by assuming a certain amount and type of supply-side effects that stem from aggregate improvement of various types of infrastructure, private investment, and upgrading of human capital. None of those takes specifically into account the effects that individual energy projects financed by CSF are going to have on the availability, supply and quality of the various types of energy fuels.

More specifically, during the last four years a number of activities, which are co-financed by the European Commission and the Greek government, are being implemented within the framework of the Operational Programmes for Energy, Industry and Environmental Protection. Some of these actions will play an important role in the efforts to restrict the overall growth of emissions of greenhouse gases in Greece.[35] These actions can be distinguished to those directly related to improvements of the energy system and to those that primarily target towards environmental protection in Greece including:

- energy efficiency improvements in the electricity sector and promotion of RES
- interventions in the industrial sector through the use of more energy efficient production procedures, application of best available techniques and technologies and increased use of RES
- interventions in the transportation sector through the shift towards less polluting forms of transport, improvement of the energy efficiency of vehicles, improvements in road networks and the continuous renewal of the road vehicle fleet, and protection and enhancement of forests.

Furthermore, the implementation of the third phase of the CSF is expected to begin in 2000. Some of its priorities, related to the energy sector, will be the extension of the NG pipeline network, the interconnection with electricity networks of neighbouring countries, further promotion of RES and co-generation, voluntary agreements with the industrial sector for the promotion of energy efficiency, promotion of the rational use of energy and other infrastructure improvements. Such interventions would enhance the flexibility and the competitiveness of the Greek energy system, thus assisting in effectively meeting requirements arising from the liberalisation of the energy market in Europe. Although not all of these activities are explicitly targeted towards the reduction of greenhouse gases, they are expected to drive CO_2 emissions to a much lower level by the period 2008-2012.

Finally, the provision of the Kyoto Protocol concerning the consideration of a basket of 6 gases constitutes an element of 'flexibility' for the identification of the most cost-effective and environmentally sound policies. Predicted growth rates of CO_2 emissions, indicate that apart from any efforts related to energy sector activities there is also a need in identifying measures that would reduce significantly emissions of other gases (particularly fluorinated compounds with high global warming potential). There is, therefore, much scope for the prompt start in the identification and implementation of such initiatives to ensure compliance with the commitments assumed by the end of the 2008-2012 period.

Chapter 6

EPILOGUE: POLICY LESSONS FOR THE FUTURE

According to economic theory and empirical findings, a country that experiences a low rate of growth and a relatively low public to private capital ratio can generate higher growth by increasing public capital formation. Increased infrastructure raises the marginal product of private capital and induces private investment. Thus, the country can attain a higher long-run growth rate of output. This justifies the use of transfers for public capital formation promoted by aid policies, which aim at fostering growth in less developed countries. An inflow of funds for public capital formation will speed up the process of growth and convergence.

In the case of the CSF funds inflows to Greece, the universal conclusion reached here is that in the absence of positive supply-side effects generated by CSF actions, all types of these actions produce only a temporary rise in activity and employment. The estimates presented here show that, under certain assumptions, a fall in output growth rate accompanies the cessation of the programme. So, after the implementation period, the economy returns to the course that would have been the case without the funds. A permanent rise in growth, activity and employment is achieved only when CSF generates positive supply-side effects.

Such a conclusion may not be seen as surprising, given the disappointing experience of the first CSF. Being allocated mainly to a multitude of small-scale projects and uncoordinated actions, and driven mainly by the haste to absorb funds the first CSF had few lasting effects. The economy grew faster in 1990 and 1991, but then activity slackened. A similar picture emerges as a possible outcome for the second CSF if the effects are left to operate only through the demand side.

However, if supply-side effects are assumed to operate even at a moderate scale, the picture changes starkly. Total output will be rising for a long period of time, and a decade after the end of CSF the economy will still be growing at a faster rate than in the absence of EU financing; productivity, employment and the exporting capacity of the country will improve accordingly.

This finding has far-reaching implications for the allocation, implementation and monitoring of the Plan, since it calls for actions that ensure the maximum possible efficiency if a lasting improvement is to occur in the economy. National and EU authorities should make sure that the following conditions are satisfied in order to achieve the supply-side effects envisaged in the *ex ante* analysis of CSF:

- design, construction, and operation of hard infrastructure projects after a careful examination of the benefits that are going to accrue to the various sectors of economic activity. The hard infrastructure actions of the Regional Programmes should be implemented in conjunction with national-scale ones so that supplementarity rather than repetition is achieved.
- the implementation of soft infrastructure actions should take into account the demand that is likely to develop for such services (e.g. R&D, culture, health, etc). The concentration on top-down activities that cannot attract substantial demand from the production and service sector should be avoided.
- training and education should be geared to providing skills in current and future demand by the economic activities, so that their effect is felt on improving the productivity of the human factor.
- the implementation of the Programme should ensure that all envisaged co-financing by the private sector is realised, so that the maximum impact on investment and infrastructure utilisation is achieved.

An important question that arises though is whether the increased growth rates implied by such policies could be sustained after the ending of transfers from abroad. The ending of transfers will be associated with a higher *output level* and a higher *public capital stock*. But in order to maintain the increased *growth rates* the recipient country will have to continue financing permanently higher public investment through domestic resources or, otherwise, it will experience a 'hard landing' effect at the terminal period.

It seems that, given the nature and size of Plans financed by Structural Funds (which involve mainly large-scale projects), the private sector would never engage in financing this type of infrastructure investment; however, increased infrastructure raises the expected return of private capital and induces private investment. Therefore, in the case of Greece, aid via Structural Funds is of crucial importance for achieving the goal of real convergence with the rest of the European countries.

Financial assistance through Structural Funds in Europe becomes more important in light of the regional policy reforms agreed in March 1999 in the Berlin Summit. European leaders agreed to allocate 213 bn Euros to funds for regional aid from 2000 to 2006 comparing to 203 bn Euros over the 1993-1999 period. The allocation among member states shall be based on the percent of population eligible for assistance, on regional and national welfare criteria and the degree of structural deficiencies, and particularly unemployment.[36] In particular, Greece is expected to receive 24.9 bn Euros for the 2000-2006 period, compared to 21.9 bn Euros for the 1993-1999 period.

An important question that remains open, though, concerns the fungibility of foreign assistance. If an investment project would be undertaken even in the absence of foreign financing, then foreign aid may release resources for other purposes, thus ending up in financing undesirable activities (Devarajan and Swaroop, 1998). Therefore, foreign aid should not alter public investment policies, but rather increase the amount available for investment. This will increase the rate of return on infrastructure and overall utility, as it may allow the design and implementation of larger-scale projects.

Financial assistance of the type provided by the Structural Funds can also improve the social infrastructure of the economy. Hall and Jones (1999) argue that the large variations in output per capita across countries can only partially be explained by differences in physical and human capital. On the contrary, these authors show that social infrastructure, in the form of '*..institutions and government policies that determine the economic environment*', plays a crucial role in explaining variations in per capita income. The legislative and institutional framework affects the level and productivity of key inputs and provides favorable conditions for sustainable development.

To this extent, assistance through the Structural Funds provides a stable framework for long-term growth by promoting a number of institutional changes and structural reforms in critical areas of economic activity. Also, public consensus on the beneficial role of the EU in these countries underlines the usefulness of membership and renders the acceptance of common European policies easier.

Today, a large regional market of 60-70 million people in South-eastern Europe is being shaped, with significant opportunities for co-operation and trade. The main characteristic of this new market is potential economic relations between bordering countries. This opportunity is related to the prospect of re-composing the economic space in its vicinity with the creation of a regional Balkan market, in which it will have a central and highly influential role. For the first time in the post-war period, a real opportunity is given to the Balkan countries to interact without political or military barriers, leaving the level and type of their trade relations to be determined by markets and geography.

Therefore, as regards the EU and Structural Funds, policies promoting economic unification and coherence of the South-eastern European economic space are necessary and should include support for the following:

- encourage all Balkan countries to the perspective of joining EU, according to the progress they make.
- promote a strategic development plan for the Balkan region at various regional and sectoral levels with emphasis on intra-regional co-operation and integration. This plan should include the financing of

transportation and telecommunication networks that will allow the integration of existing development areas in the Balkans and reveal the role of South-eastern Europe as an emerging regional market with significant size, strong intra-regional relations and efficient infrastructure, providing a strategic advantage for boosting EU economic relations in the Black Sea, Eastern Mediterranean and the Middle East regions.

Appendix

THE GREEK ECONOMY MODEL

This Appendix contains a brief survey of existing macromodelling work for the Greek economy, which is followed by the four-sector macroeconometric model estimates for each sector (used in chapter 3), together with the model identities and the data description. It also includes the energy model estimates and identities, as well as the energy data description (outlined in chapter 5).

The model description is given in four sections. The first section discusses the supply side of the model, presenting the estimated factor demand equations for each sector, followed by the wage and price formation processes. The second section deals with the demand side of the model, focusing on consumption, exports and government revenues. The presentation of the econometric model for the Greek economy closes in the third section with the model identities. Finally, the fourth section presents the estimates of sectoral energy demand, the formation of energy prices, and the linkages between the two models.

Standard errors for the individual parameters in the estimated sections are given in parentheses. Several equations are estimated in the two-stage error-correction form (Engle and Granger, 1987). First, the long-run equation estimates are reported (accompanied by the Adjusted R-Squared and the Adjusted Dickey-Fuller unit root test on the residuals) and then the residual (Z) from the long-run equation is used as an explanatory variable in the short-run equation.

The statistical misspecifation tests following each equation are the following: DW-statistic is the Durbin-Watson test for autocorrelation of order one, the Durbin's *h* is the autocorrelation test with lagged dependent variable, the Breusch Godfrey test is for AR/MA processes in the residuals of order 1, the White test is for heteroscedasticity, the Augmented (1 lag) Dickey-Fuller is for a unit root test in the cointegrating residuals, the Engle ARCH test is for autoregressive conditional heteroscedasticity, the Chow test is for parameter stability and the Jarque-Bera test is for normality. Probability values are in brackets. More details on these misspecification tests can be found in Spanos (1986) and Banerjee et al. (1993).

1. MODELLING THE SUPPLY SIDE

Numerous econometric studies have attempted to model the production process in the Greek economy. The studies are divided according to whether they model aggregate economic activity or specific sectors, and also according to the questions they address. During the 1970s and the 1980s the focal point was the extent of substitutability between capital and labour in Greece, especially in the manufacturing sector. Later studies extended the two-factor framework to include energy and intermediate materials, while other emphasised the role of cyclical effects on the utilisation of production factors.

Earlier econometric estimates of firms' behaviour focused on the issue of substitution between capital and labour. This question appeared to be particularly pressing in a period in which Greek manufacturing started showing a serious decline in productivity, as a result of the oil shock in 1973 and the structural changes following the overthrow of dictatorship in 1974.

Lianos (1975) used data on large and medium-scale manufacturing in Greece over the period 1958-1969 to estimate a CES production function with capital and labour augmentation factors. Lacking the appropriate data for the capital stock he used the inverted form suggested by Arrow et al. (1961) and found that the elasticity of substitution between capital and labour systematically exceeds unity. The finding was confirmed by both cross-section and time-series estimates for two-digit sectors of Greek manufacturing. Lianos took these findings to suggest that there is no fixity of factors in Greek manufacturing; thus, increasing the capital intensity of production should be preferred over policies aiming to increase labour supply, given the shortage of skilled workers in Greece.

In a sequel paper, Lianos (1976) concentrated on the issue of factor augmentation in large-scale manufacturing, and reported that the rate of growth in the efficiency of capital is 9% per annum compared with only 4% in labour. Thus, technical progress should not be treated as Hicks-neutral. Moreover, when these results are combined with the large elasticity of substitution, they are taken to suggest that technical progress in Greek manufacturing is labour-saving and capital-using.

The above findings were subsequently challenged by a number of studies. Kintis (1977) estimated a similarly inverted CES production function for three-digit sectors and concluded that the elasticity of substitution should not be very different than unity. Ioannides and Caramanis (1979) employed the cost function approach and found that the elasticity of substitution is considerably lower than one. In such a case, policies favouring a reduction in real wages and greater flexibility in the labour market would be preferable. Caramanis (1981) reiterated with estimates of a cost function for the textiles and chemical sectors, in which labour input was disaggregated into unskilled, technical, and white-collar workers. The substitution elasticity between capital and labour was found significantly lower than unity and not very different for the various types of labour, thus strongly suggesting separability of the two factors of production. Elasticity of substitution of various types of labour was found to be considerable between the first two groups and the last two, but not between the first and the third ones.

In all the above studies, utilisation of factors was assumed to be full and this perhaps led to serious misspecifications with respect to the contribution of each factor over the business cycle. To avoid this problem, Papatheodorou (1991) assumes variable factor utilisation and estimates a nested CES function with a putty/semi-putty structure of capital and energy in the inner process and a combination of labour in efficiency units and a capital-energy bundle in the outer process. Including variables such as the level of sales, unit costs, and the inventory gap to indicate the degree of factor utilisation, he finds that the elasticity of substitution between capital and labour is below unity (0.94). Ignoring the cyclical effects, the elasticity is found considerably higher (1.34). Although obtained for the aggregate economic activity, the latter figure is surprisingly close to estimates reached by Lianos (1975) for large-scale-manufacturing. Thus the role of cyclical effects perhaps can be used to explain some of the differences in the estimates of the elasticity of substitution.

Georgoutsos (1992) provides estimates of factor demands for the manufacturing sector by assuming that firms choose capital and labour to maximise the expected discounted stream of profits subject to a Cobb-Douglas production constraint. Technical progress is assumed neutral in the Hicksian sense. The estimation yields the intensity of labour equal to 0.74, close to the historically observed average share of labour income. The assumption of constant returns to scale cannot be rejected. He also finds that labour input should be better represented in the production function by manhours, rather than the number of employees, because, in the latter case, the contribution of employment to the change of output is overestimated over the business cycle. This confirms the findings of Papatheodorou (1991) on the importance of cyclical effects in the supply of output. Constant returns to scale are also confirmed by Zanias (1991).

Finally, another question concerns the economies of scale. All previously mentioned studies assume constant returns to scale, but this is challenged by Garganas (1992) who establishes that increasing returns to scale are present in the aggregate economy; more details are given latter where his macroeconometric model is outlined. A possible explanation of such diverse findings may be found in the results of Christodoulakis and Segoura (1993), who estimate a Cobb-Douglas production function with both private and public factors of production, as in Aschauer (1989). Returns to scale are found to be constant over private inputs, but increasing when the public capital stock is also treated as a factor of production. In their estimates, utilisation rate accounts for cyclical effects thus the assumption of unit elasticity of substitution is broadly in agreement with the findings of Papatheodorou (1991). Furthermore, the coefficient of labour intensity is similar to that reported by Georgoutsos (1992).

Most econometric studies estimate demand for employment as a simple Keynesian function of aggregate demand and labour-saving technical progress. Karadeloglou and Koutsouvelis (1991) apply this form separately for wage earners and self-employed. Output elasticity is found to be 0.80 for the former case, suggesting the existence of small costs in adjusting the level of employment in response to output changes, and 0.95 for the latter so that such costs are negligible in the self-employed sector. Technical progress is found significant in both cases.

Lolos and Zonzilos (1992) reach different conclusions by choosing to include a real wage term that affects negatively the demand for dependent employment, and ignore the role of labour-saving progress. Real wage elasticity is found to be very strong (0.70), while output elasticity is now 1.10 suggesting negligible adjustment costs in changing employment. However, this contradicts other findings according to which there is a considerable degree of labour hoarding practices in Greece, and several inflexibilities in the labour market are still in place. Regarding self-employment, Lolos and Zonzilos (1992) report an equation with an output elasticity of 0.40, which may be thought of as surprisingly low given the absence of rigidities in this sector.

Other models also offer estimates of sectoral employment. Koutsouvelis and Anastassakou (1989) employ the same simple Keynesian form described above, augmented by a lagged employment term to indicate the adjustment process. Results seem to indicate that agricultural employment is completely hysteretic (the lagged term coefficient is equal to one), inelastic to changes in output and with no falling time trend. All of them, however, appear to be at odds with reality, given that agricultural population in Greece is trend-falling and shows considerable variation between successive periods of low and high land fertility. The lowest output elasticity is reported for the energy sector (0.22), while the highest (0.78) is found in the service sector where self-employment is very extensive.

Capros et al. (1988) obtain demand for labour in manufacturing by estimating an inverted production function that has already been discussed. For labour demand in the service sector, the simple Keynesian scheme is adopted with total hours of work as the dependent variable. In sharp disagreement with Karadeloglou and Koutsouvelis (1991) they find that the long-run output elasticity is only 0.23, while the time trend is positive.

In Garganas (1992), demand for employment is estimated as an inverted production function, depending on the level of activity and relative factor prices. Okun's Law seems to hold in all cases in the long-run studies. One percent rise in activity generates a long-run increase of 0.50% in business sector employment, 0.44% in manufacturing and 0.42% in self-employment.

The supply-side of the new model consists of four sectors: tradable, non-tradable, public and agricultural. The tradable sector consists of the manufacturing and mining sectors, while the non-tradable sector consists of electricity, trade, transport, communications, construction, housing and banking activities. It should be noted here that, under this definition, the non-tradable sector includes tourism and shipping (under transport); these sectors are rather sensitive to world fluctuations since they are highly competitive and open to global market conditions. However, they are also closely linked (especially tourism) to developments in the national economy whilst they do not account for more than 10% of total non-tradable sector output.

Moreover, the modelling of a more disaggregate economy structure would be of little use for the evaluation of the CSF effects as analytical data for the CSF subprogrammes (including the national and private co-financing ratios for these actions) are not yet officially available. The disaggregation of the model and the definition of the tradable and non-tradable sectors broadly follow those of the HERMIN models for Ireland, Portugal and Spain. Tradable and non-tradable sectors are of particular importance in the HERMIN models since they constitute the main operating channels for an intervention such as the CSF (see also Bradley et al., 1995a, pp.234-235, and chapter 3).

We describe a theoretical framework for the derivation of the factor demand equations. Assume that each firm maximises profits intertemporally subject to the production function with constant returns to scale constraint (see also Modesto and Neves, 1995):

$$\max \sum_{t=0}^{\infty} (\beta^t \{p_t Y_t - w_t L_t - i_t I_t\})$$

subject to $Y_t = A\{\beta[\exp(\lambda_L t)L_t]^{-\rho} + (1-\beta)\,[\exp(\lambda_E t)I_t]^{-\rho}\}^{-1/\rho}$

where p_t is the price level, Y_t is real output, w_t is the nominal wage rate, L_t is labour, i_t is the nominal cost of investment and I_t is investment.

Parameter values are denoted by A (scale parameter), $\sigma=1/(1+\rho)$ is the elasticity of substitution, and λ_L and λ_I are the rates of technical progress associated with labor and investment respectively. Note that investment enters directly as a factor in the production function. Factor demand equations are given by:

$$logL_t = a_1 + logY_t - \sigma logRPL_t - (1-\sigma)\lambda_L t$$

$$logI_t^* = a_2 + logY_t - \sigma logRPK_t - (1-\sigma)\lambda_I t$$

where RPL_t and RPI_t are the real price of labor and investment respectively. Assuming now that the optimal investment in every period I_t^* given by the factor demand equation is adjusted in the following way:

$$logI_t = (1-\psi)logI_{t-1} + \psi logI_t^*$$

After replacing in the factor demand equation we finally obtain that investment is given by the following formula:

$$logI_t = \psi a_2 + (1-\psi)logI_{t-1} + \psi logY_t - \psi\sigma logRPK_t - \psi(1-\sigma)\lambda_I t$$

The output of the tradable sector is modelled as a function of aggregate domestic expenditure in the economy and world output. The growth rate of tradable sector output is determined by changes in domestic spending with an elasticity of 0.53 and world activity (proxied by total output in OECD countries) with an elasticity of 0.97. The relatively high value of the world output elasticity can be explained by the degree of openness of the Greek economy; for instance, as reported by Dimeli et al. (1997) the elasticity of output in Greece with respect to output in the EU is 0.62. The specification was extended to include a measure of competitiveness proxied by the lagged change in the ratio of domestic to EU unit labour cost with an elasticity of -0.29. Non-tradable sector output is modelled as a function of aggregate domestic expenditure, but is also found to depend to a small extent on the volume of exports to account for export-generated services (such as transport, communications, banking, etc.); the elasticities being 0.57 and 0.10 respectively.

For both the tradable and non-tradable sectors, demand for labour (also derived by intertemporal maximisation of profits as described above) is modelled by using real factor prices as explanatory variables. The long-run elasticity of employment with respect to the corresponding real wage rate (proxied as a ratio of the hourly wage in manufacturing to the sectoral price index) is found to be -0.06 in the tradable sector. The corresponding elasticity for the non-tradable sector (where the real wage rate is proxied by the ratio of employees' compensation to the sectoral price index) is found to be -0.12.

As far as investment is concerned, a partial adjustment scheme is assumed, according to which investment is a function of lagged levels, the real price of capital and sectoral output. The user cost of capital in the investment equations for the tradable and non-tradable sectors is proxied by the nominal interest rate in manufacturing and trade respectively, plus the average depreciation rate minus the inflation rate of the private investment deflator. The expression is then multiplied by the ratio of private investment deflator to GDP deflator. The elasticity of investment with respect to output is larger in the tradable sector (0.95) than in the non-tradable sector (0.37). In the latter, a large part of investment consists of public capital formation.

1.1. Tradable Sector

Demand for investment:

$$\log QITR = \underset{(1.278)}{-1.328} + \underset{(0.212)}{0.607}*\log QITR(-1) - \underset{(0.027)}{0.049}*\log RPKTR(-1) + \underset{(0.312)}{0.563}*\log YTR(-1)$$

Adjusted R-squared = 0.469
Breusch/Godfrey LM (AR/MA1) = 0.531 [0.466]
ARCH test = 1.148 [0.284]
Chow test = 1.379 [0.303]
White het. test = 8.920 [0.445]
Jarque-Bera normality test = 1.110 [0.574]

Demand for labour:

$$\log LTR = \underset{(0.114)}{2.203} - \underset{(0.033)}{0.060}*\log[WMFH(-1)/PTR(-1)] + \log YTR$$

Adjusted R-squared = 0.106
Breusch/Godfrey LM (AR/MA1) = 1.505 [0.220]
ARCH test = 0.006 [0.937]
Chow test = 1.793 [0.197]
White het. test = 0.913 [0.633]
Jarque-Bera normality test = 1.081 [0.582]

Determination of output:

$$\Delta logYTR = \underset{(0.223)}{0.532}*\Delta logQSP - \underset{(0.071)}{0.292}*\Delta log[ULC(-1)/ULCEC(-1)] + \underset{(0.299)}{0.967}*\Delta logWGDP$$

Adjusted R-squared = 0.660
Breusch/Godfrey LM (AR/MA1) = -0.038 [1.000]
ARCH test = 0.870 [0.351]
Chow test = 1.083 [0.390]
White het. test = 9.314 [0.409]
Jarque-Bera normality test = 1.702 [0.427]

1.2. Non-Tradable Sector

Demand for labour:

$$logLNT = \underset{(0.817)}{2.973} - \underset{(0.099)}{0.123}*log(WTRD/PNT) - \underset{(0.003)}{0.007}*T74 + logYNT$$

Adjusted R-squared = 0.758
Breusch/Godfrey LM (AR/MA1) = 3.505 [0.061]
ARCH test = 1.038 [0.308]
Chow test = 0.345 [0.044]
White het. test = 3.827 [0.574]
Jarque-Bera normality test = 2.536 [0.281]

Demand for investment:

$$logQINT = \underset{(0.810)}{0.553} + \underset{(0.171)}{0.613}*logQINT(-1) - \underset{(0.051)}{0.057}*logRPKNT + \underset{(0.182)}{0.228}*logYNT$$

Adjusted R-squared = 0.530
Breusch/Godfrey LM (AR/MA1) = 1.786 [0.181]
ARCH test = 0.202 [0.653]
Chow test = 2.262 [0.123]
White het. test = 8.847 [0.452]
Jarque-Bera normality test = 1.212 [0.545]

Determination of output:

$$\Delta logYNT = 0.008 + 0.570*\Delta logQSP + 0.103*\Delta logQX$$
$$\quad\quad\quad (0.005)\ (0.116)\quad\quad\quad (0.036)$$

Adjusted R-squared = 0.614
Breusch/Godfrey LM (AR/MA1) = 0.263 [0.608]
ARCH test = 2.105 [0.147]
Chow test = 0.408 [0.750]
White het. test = 6.293 [0.279]
Jarque-Bera normality test = 1.045 [0.593]

1.3. Public Sector

The public sector expanded dramatically in Greece during the 1980s, with general government expenditure rising from 35% in 1980 to 62% of GDP in 1992; Christodoulakis (1994b) reviews fiscal developments in Greece after 1974. Despite the dominant role it plays in economic activity, attempts to model the behaviour of the public sector are scant and far from providing a comprehensive presentation and explanation of its functions.

Most econometric models treat government spending on consumption and investment as exogenous, and usually provide estimates for the various types of state revenues. Such a distinct treatment seems to be justified by the fact that expenditure items are used as decision variables by the government, and then the tax system is designed in such a way as to produce the revenues to finance a predetermined level of spending. In support of this view, Provopoulos and Zambaras (1991) and Kollias and Makrydakis (1995) reached the conclusion that causation runs only from the latter to the former.

Estimates for government expenditure concern only a few items. Garganas (1992) provided equations for interest payments, the operating costs of public enterprises, and the wage bill. Karadeloglou and Koutsouvelis (1991) estimated equations for pensions and some welfare allowances. All other spending items are treated as exogenous.

In the present setting, public output is modeled as a function of public consumption. In turn, the latter is considered to be a function of the number of persons working in the public sector and the real wage rate in the public sector.

In the public sector, output and consumption are modelled in the two-step error correction form. Behavioural modelling of the public sector is deemed necessary as the control of public expenditure in constant terms is closely associated to the achievement of economic policy goals, such as the reduction of inflation and public debt. Therefore, it would be useful to obtain estimates of the long- and short-run response of output and expenditure in the public sector with respect to public employment and wages. Notice here that an alternative route for modeling public expenditure would be through a national account identity linking expenditure with the wage bill, but such a relationship would ignore the impact of public employment and the real wage rate on public expenditure.

The long-run equation for public output (consisting of administration, health, education, and other services) reveals that it is determined mainly by public consumption with an elasticity of 0.76. The corresponding short-run elasticity is found to be 0.52. In turn, public consumption depends in the long run on the number of civil servants employed and the real wage rate with the corresponding elasticities being 0.29 and 0.59. Short-run elasticities are found to be 0.38 and 0.41 respectively.

Public sector output:

Long-run equation:

$$\log YPS = 1.145 + 0.764*\log QCG$$
$$\quad (0.071) \quad (0.016)$$

Adjusted R-squared = 0.991
Augmented Dickey-Fuller = -3.394 [0.080]

Short-run equation:

$$\Delta\log YPS = 0.007 + 0.526*\Delta\log QCG - 0.712*Z(-1)$$
$$\quad (0.004) \quad (0.098) \qquad\qquad (0.212)$$

Adjusted R-squared = 0.627
Breusch/Godfrey LM (AR/MA1) = 1.747 [0.186]
ARCH test = 0.168 [0.681]
Chow test = 0.982 [0.429]
White het. test = 3.195 [0.670]
Jarque-Bera normality test = 1.913 [0.384]

Public consumption:

Long-run equation:

$$\log QCG = 0.232 + 0.294*\log LPS + 0.593*\log(WPUB/PPS)$$
$$\quad (0.221) \quad (0.098) \qquad\qquad (0.123)$$

Adjusted R-squared = 0.972
Augmented Dickey-Fuller = -3.312 [0.093]

Short-run equation:

$$\Delta logQCG=\underset{(0.009)}{0.005}+\underset{(0.203)}{0.386}*\Delta logLPS+\underset{(0.135)}{0.414}*\Delta log(WPUB/PPS)-\underset{(0.159)}{0.525}*Z(-1)$$

Adjusted R-squared = 0.500
Breusch/Godfrey LM (AR/MA1) = 0.484 [0.486]
ARCH test = 0.071 [0.790]
Chow test = 5.475 [0.010]
White het. test = 7.845 [0.550]
Jarque-Bera normality test = 1.508 [0.471]

1.4. The Agricultural Sector

Finally, output in the agricultural sector is estimated through a Cobb-Douglas production function of labour and the agricultural capital stock with constant returns to scale. Estimates are obtained using average productivity of labour as the dependent variable. To account for the fact that output is a flow during the period while the capital stock is an end-of-period variable, the mid-year capital stock is used in the estimation. The assumption of constant returns to scale is accepted by the data. Estimation produced a capital stock coefficient of 0.68, leading to a share of remunerated labour of 0.32. The small size of the share can be explained by the fact that the family of the farmer provides most of employment in agriculture and only a small portion of agricultural income is recorded as remuneration to outside employees. As indicated by the negative sign of the time-trend coefficient, agricultural population in Greece is falling, although it shows considerable variation between successive periods of low and high fertility.

Production function:

$$log(YAG/LAGR) = \underset{(0.139)}{-1.168} + \underset{(0.071)}{0.843}*log[0.5*(QKA(-1) + QKA(-2))/LAGR(-1)]$$

Adjusted R-squared = 0.887
Breusch/Godfrey LM (AR/MA1) = 3.797 [0.051]
ARCH test = 1.821 [0.177]
Chow test = 0.621 [0.550]
White het. test = 0.379 [0.827]
Jarque-Bera normality test = 0.125 [0.939]

Agricultural employment:

$$\log(LAGR/POP) = \underset{(0.353)}{-0.651} + \underset{(0.181)}{0.676}*\log[LAGR(-1)/POP(-1)] - \underset{(0.005)}{0.009}*T74$$

Adjusted R-squared = 0.973
Breusch/Godfrey LM (AR/MA1) = 0.006 [0.937]
ARCH test = 0.179 [0.672]
Chow test = 2.463 [0.105]
White het. test = 8.911 [0.113]
Jarque-Bera normality test = 4.056 [0.132]

Investment in agriculture depends on the user cost of capital (proxied by the interest rate on agricultural credit) and last period's investment. Results show that only the interest rate is a significant determinant of investment, and this can be explained by the fact that interest rates for loans to the agricultural sector were administratively determined for most of the period. Moreover, credit was extended to farmers through government controlled banks (Sakellariou and Howland, 1993), thus implying that efficient credit pricing was practically absent.

Agricultural investment:

$$\log QIA = \underset{(0.590)}{1.637} + \underset{(0.207)}{0.416}*\log QIA(-1) - \underset{(0.101)}{0.239}*\log IRAG$$

Adjusted R-squared = 0.650
Breusch/Godfrey LM (AR/MA1) = 0.777 [0.378]
ARCH test = 2.306 [0129]
Chow test = 1.057 [0.398]
White het. test = 2.989 [0.702]
Jarque-Bera normality test = 0.042 [0.979]

1.5. Wage Formation

Wage setting in Greece is a highly centralised process of bargaining between the employers' federation and trade unions. Besides, the government heavily regulates the institutional framework of negotiations. The main agreement concerns minimum wages in the private sector, which is subsequently used as the basis for negotiating wages and salaries in the rest of the economy.

During the 1980s, the government had institutionalised an automatic indexation scheme, with lower wages adjusting fully with inflation while the adjustment of higher wages was below that level. The indexation scheme was postponed during the short-lived stabilisation program of 1983-84, suspended during the second stabilisation program in 1985-87, implemented again during 1988 and 1989, and finally abolished in 1990. Bargaining over the minimum wage mainly evolves around the extent of covering the losses due to past or expected inflation, but other issues concerning the level of unemployment, training and job safety have recently entered the agenda of negotiations. A further adjustment of wages, to take into account productivity of firms and profitability changes, continues at the sectoral or the firm level, at least as far as the private sector is concerned.

To obtain estimates for the wage equations, different authors have suggested various ways to take the above factors into account. Karadeloglou and Koutsouvelis (1991) estimate a simple Phillips curve with wages responding to the level of unemployment, and over-reacting to price changes (long-run elasticity 1.42). Capros et al. (1988) estimate a similar equation for the wage in the manufacturing sector and then use it as a 'guiding-post' for setting wages in the total economy. Price elasticity is found to be 1.50 for manufacturing and 2.08 in the aggregate. Strong overindexation is also implied by the disaggregated estimates of the Hermes-Greece model.

Different estimates are obtained by Garganas (1992). Wages are modelled first in the manufacturing sector, and then there is a simple catch-up process in the aggregate economy, the central administration and public enterprises. In manufacturing, wage responds only by 66% to price changes in the short-run and is fully adjusted only with some delay. Other determinants include the level of capacity utilisation in manufacturing as an indication of labour shortages, and an exogenous time trend to capture productivity gains.

To avoid the usual finding of wage overindexation in econometric estimates we estimate a Phillips-type wage rate equation for the manufacturing sector (with prices adjusted for indirect taxation), and we also include a productivity term to take account of productivity changes in total economy.

The nominal wage growth rate in the tradable sector is estimated in the form of an unemployment-augmented Phillips curve. The equation includes a term for the productivity growth rate that exerts a positive influence in wage formation with a coefficient of 0.48. The coefficient on inflation is less than unity (0.59), indicating partial indexation of wages in accordance with the institutional framework in Greece during most of the period 1974-94. Up to 1981 there was no full indexation, between 1982 and 1985 there was a formal indexation, and after 1985 the government adopted a less-than-full scheme to account only partially for the income losses due to inflation. Minimum wages in the tradable sector were fully indexed, whereas higher wages were gradually subjected to limited increases leading to an average degree below one (see also Alogoskoufis, 1990). The large value of the autonomous term (0.15) suggests that formation of nominal wages reflects to a large extent pressures of trade unions for continuous nominal wage increases. Wages in the non-tradable and the public sector follow developments in the tradable sector.

Wage rate in manufacturing:

$$\Delta \log WMFH = \underset{(0.002)}{0.154} + \underset{(0.289)}{0.593} * \Delta \log(PTR*(1+VAT)) - \underset{(0.039)}{0.009} * UUR(-1) + \underset{(0.232)}{0.478} * \Delta \log(Y/L)$$

Adjusted R-squared = 0.493
Breusch/Godfrey LM (AR/MA1) = 0.036 [0.848]
ARCH test = 3.249 [0.071]
Chow test = 0.722 [0.593]
White het. test = 11.022 [0.274]
Jarque-Bera normality test = 0.615 [0.735]

Box 11: Overindexation of wages in Greek economy models

Greek economy macromodels have attempted to estimate the wage formation process by examining the relationship with prices. In the MYKL model (Karadeloglou and Koutsouvelis, 1991) wages are found to overrespond to price changes. The long-run elasticity of wages to prices equals 1.42, whilst the effect of unemployment is rather weak.

A crucial bloc of the Hermes-Greece Model (Koutsouvelis and Anastassakou, 1989) is wage formation in each sector, which is assumed to take place along a Phillips curve with regards to aggregate unemployment. Surprisingly, all sectors display an unusually high long-run elasticity of prices (lower value 1.34, maximum 2.22, average 1.77) attributed by the authors to overindexation of wages. As in the MYKL model, the effect of unemployment on wages is rather weak.

In the Greek Economic Model of the National Technical University of Athens (Capros et al., 1988) sectoral labour productivity does not influence wages in manufacturing, despite the fact that productivity could be much better measured at a sectoral level. In contrast, productivity influences wage setting in the aggregate economy where measurement problems are presumably more severe, especially regarding the non-traded sectors. Also, the long-run elasticity of prices is unusually high (1.50 in the manufacturing sector and 2.08 for the total economy) and it is likely that this is a consequence of failing to properly take into account developments in labour productivity.

These findings, however, are in conflict with actual experience in Greece where indexation has been less than full, leading to a *decline* in the real wage rate due to the diminishing incremental adjustment for higher wages and the long-run developments in economic activity. For example, the dramatic rise in wages engineered in 1982 by the government as 'an overdue justice to low-income classes' led several firms out of business. As a result, private investment was substantially cancelled, unemployment rose and the average real wage rate in the economy fell significantly.

Another example of partial indexation occurred after the devaluation of the drachma in 1985 by 15%, which succeeded in raising exports and curtailing imports only to the extent that real wages fell, as a result of an unusually tough incomes policy. When this policy was relaxed and indexation was again introduced in 1988, competitiveness was quickly eroded and output ceased to rise any further, leading in the longer-run to a fall in productivity and real wages.

1.6. Price Deflators

Prices are modelled as functions of unit labour cost (domestic component) and the price of imports (external component). Homogeneity of degree one was imposed in the econometric estimates and accepted by the data. Changes in the nominal unit labour cost are explained by changes in the average nominal wage rate minus changes in productivity.

Wholesale price index:

$$\Delta logWPI = \underset{(0.009)}{0.005} + \underset{(0.138)}{0.497}*\Delta logULC + (1-0.497)*\Delta logPM$$

Adjusted R-squared = 0.516
DW-statistic = 1.593

Consumer price index:

$$\Delta logCPI = \underset{(0.010)}{0.012} + \underset{(0.157)}{0.617}*\Delta logULC + (1-0.619)*\Delta logPM + \underset{(0.716)}{1.022}*\Delta logVAT$$

Adjusted R-squared = 0.261
DW-statistic = 1.024

Price of exports:

$$\Delta logPX = -\underset{(0.005)}{0.039} + \underset{(0.059)}{0.804}*\Delta logULC + (1-0.804)*\Delta log(WCPI*XED) + \underset{(0.024)}{0.165}*D80$$

Adjusted R-squared = 0.8711
DW-statistic = 1.500

Public consumption deflator:

$$\Delta logPCG = \underset{(0.005)}{0.011} + \underset{(0.083)}{0.781}*\Delta logULC + (1-0.781)*\Delta logPM$$

Adjusted R-squared = 0.748
DW-statistic = 1.528

Public investment deflator:

$$\Delta\log PIG = 0.009 + 0.789{*}\Delta\log ULC + (1-0.789){*}\Delta\log PM$$
$$(0.011)\ (0.166)$$

Adjusted R-squared = 0.234
DW-statistic = 1.991

Deflator of private investment:

$$\Delta\log PIP = 0.002 + 0.717{*}\Delta\log ULC + (1-0.717){*}\Delta\log PM$$
$$(0.012)\ (0.189)$$

Adjusted R-squared = 0.061
DW-statistic = 1.640

Output deflator of tradable sector:

$$\Delta\log PTR = 0.004 + 0.549{*}\Delta\log ULC + (1-0.549){*}\Delta\log PM$$
$$(0.009)\ (0.138)$$

Adjusted R-squared = 0.461
DW-statistic = 1.552

Output deflator of non-tradable sector:

$$\Delta\log PNT = -\ 0.003 + 0.805{*}\Delta\log ULC + (1-0.805){*}\Delta\log PM$$
$$(0.008)\ (0.148)$$

Adjusted R-squared = 0.211
DW-statistic = 1.410

Output deflator of public sector:

$$\Delta\log PPS = 0.018 + 0.853{*}\Delta\log ULC + (1-0.853){*}\Delta\log PM$$
$$(0.006)\ (0.099)$$

Adjusted R-squared = 0.636
DW-statistic = 1.456

Output deflator of agricultural sector:

$$\Delta\log PYA = -0.001 + 0.905{*}\Delta\log ULC + (1-0.905){*}\Delta\log PM$$
$$(0.010)\ (0.154)$$

Adjusted R-squared = 0.461
DW-statistic = 2.409

1.7. Capital Accumulation Equations

Private capital accumulation:

QKP = (1-0.029)*QKP(-1) + QTP + QINT
(0.000)

Adjusted R-squared = 0.999

Public capital accumulation:

QKG = (1-0.032)*QKG(-1) + QIG
(0.000)

Adjusted R-squared = 0.999

Agricultural capital accumulation:

QKA = (1-0.029)*QKA(-1) + QIA
(0.000)

Adjusted R-squared = 0.999

2. MODELLING THE DEMAND SIDE

2.1. Private Consumption And Wealth Effects

Private consumption is the largest component of aggregate demand and its estimation is of crucial importance to all macroeconomic models. Consumption during the post-war period in Greece follows a smooth and steadily rising trajectory, even in periods of output stagnation. In a study of the business cycle in Greece, Christodoulakis et al. (1995) report that consumption variability over a non-stationary trend is only 1.32%, much lower than output variability which is found to be 2.60%. This finding points to the 'consumption-smoothing' hypothesis, according to which the consumption decisions by households are taken on the basis of life-cycle income and/or the stock of wealth, and do not exclusively depend on currently disposable income.

However, the majority of macroeconomic models currently available in Greece does not take wealth effects into account and simply estimate consumption as a function of income. Wealth effects may be traced only indirectly through the real balance effect, which is represented by including the inflation rate as an explanatory variable. An interest rate term is also included to indicate intertemporal substitution.

Most of the estimates adopt the error-correction form to ensure a unit long-run elasticity of income. The short-run elasticity, however, is found to be remarkably low. According to various studies, short-run elasticity is reported to in the vicinity of 0.40. In the absence of wealth effects, this size is implausibly low since it implies that a change in income is translated to a lower change in private consumption by around only 40%, gradually moving to an equiproportional change in the long-run. Moreover, such a low process is not confirmed by historical evidence. For example, the average annual growth rate of output during the recent period 1980-97 has been 1.1%, while consumption was increasing by 2.0% annually in average, suggesting a faster- not a slower-response than output.

All estimates find important real balance effects. Similarly, interest rates are invariably found to exert a negative influence on consumption in Greece, due to the presence of intertemporal substitution effects and/or credit constraints, which become more binding with higher interest rates.

Private consumption is obtained as a function of disposable and private sector wealth (expressed as the sum of financial wealth and the private capital stock). The marginal propensities of consumption with respect to disposable income and wealth sum up to 0.69, a figure not far from that obtained by Sakellariou and Howland (1993) which is 0.54 for Greece. It is higher than other estimates in empirical studies of consumption which do not include the wealth effect. Private sector real financial wealth is also dependent on disposable income with an elasticity of 1.48.

The other domestic component of demand is inventories, modelled as a ratio to last period's economic activity through a partial adjustment mechanism. The ratio is found to depend on the growth rate of output as an indication of aggregate demand. Factor-cost adjustment is the net of indirect taxes on private consumption and investment minus subsidies on exports.

Real private consumption:

$$\Delta \log QCP = \underset{(0.005)}{0.007} + \underset{(0.143)}{0.354}*\Delta \log[QGDP-(TXD/CPI)] + \underset{(0.158)}{0.338}*\Delta \log QFWP$$

Adjusted R-squared = 0.549
Breusch/Godfrey LM (AR/MA1) = 0.077 [0.782]
ARCH test = 0.255 [0.613]
Chow test = 2.193 [0.134]
White het, Test = 4.628 [0.463]
Jarque-Bera normality test = 0.100 [0.951]

Personal wealth accumulation:

$$\Delta logQFWP = \underset{(0.020)}{0.018} + \underset{(0.641)}{1.480}*\Delta log[QGDP-(TXD/CPI)]$$

Adjusted R-squared = 0.185
Breusch/Godfrey LM (AR/MA1) = 1.205 [0.272]
ARCH test = 0.475 [0.490]
Chow test = 1.561 [0.240]
White het. test = 1.847 [0.397]
Jarque-Bera normality test = 0.884 [0.643]

Inventories to GDP ratio:

$$QD/QGDP(-1) = \underset{(0.003)}{0.003} + \underset{(0.099)}{0.476}*[QD(-1)/QGDP(-2)] + \underset{(0.079)}{0.372}*\Delta logQGDP$$

Adjusted R-squared = 0.778
Breusch/Godfrey LM (AR/MA1) = 0.091 [0.763]
ARCH test = 0.557 [0.455]
Chow test = 1.796 [0.198]
White het. test = 2.970 [0.705]
Jarque-Bera normality test = 0.393 [0.821]

2. 2. Export functions

Existing econometric studies obtain estimates of exports as a function of foreign demand and relative prices. They differ according to the degree of sectoral disaggregation, the speed of adjustment and the extent to which Greek producers are price-takers in the world markets. Karadeloglou and Koutsouvelis (1991) estimate separate demand functions for exported goods, tourism, and the other categories. Long-run foreign demand elasticity is found to be 0.69, 1.13 and 1.52 for the above three types of exports respectively, while price elasticities are 1.26 and 3.5 for the first two. The model contains export equations disaggregated into seven sectors. The highest demand elasticity is found for the agricultural sector (equal to 2.3) and the lowest in the exports of manufactured goods (0.19). Price elasticities are found extremely high in agriculture (4.20) and very low in the energy sector (0.30).

In the model, we introduce an explicit wealth term which is found to be significant at the 5% level. Exports of goods and services are modelled in the two-step error-correction form as a function of world activity, proxied by output in OECD countries. Elasticities of exports to changes in foreign demand are 2.48 and 2.41 in the long- and short-run respectively. These estimates are significantly higher than the ones reported by Garganas (1992) -which are 1.43 in the long-run for the goods sector and 1.61 for the service sector, and by Halikias (1988) which are 1.55 for total exports and 1.81 for manufactures. However, their equations are estimated over past sampling periods (1958-1988 in the first study and 1961-1985 in the second) when exports, which mainly consisted of strongly state-subsidised products, were less elastic to developments in the world markets. During the last two decades trade barriers were gradually lifted (particularly after Greece's entry to the EU in 1981), so that exports have become more sensitive to world demand. Moreover, similar equations estimated for other small open European economies also report high export elasticities, such as 2.18 for Spain (Herce and Sosvilla-Rivero, 1995) and 1.95 for Portugal (Modesto and Neves, 1995). Imports are determined residually to ensure the closing of the model (see Bradley et al, 1995c). The Drachma/Euro nominal exchange rate is modelled as a function of nominal unit labour cost differentials between Greece and the EU as a proxy for responding to erosion of competitiveness brought about by unequal price developments in Greece and competitor countries. The estimated coefficient is not significantly different than one; thus we postulate a unit coefficient when the model is used for forecasting, in order to ensure that projections are not biased by steady erosion of competitiveness. Finally, imports are treated as a residual of total demand.

Exports:

Long-run equation:

$$\log QX = -18.245 + 2.482 * \log WGDP$$
$$\quad (0.751) \quad (0.081)$$

Adjusted R-squared = 0.979
Augmented Dickey-Fuller = -3.078 [0.138]

Short-run equation:

$$\Delta \log QX = 0.005 + 2.407 * \Delta \log WGDP - 0.664 * Z(-1)$$
$$\quad (0.026) \quad (0.906) \qquad\qquad (0.219)$$

Adjusted R-squared = 0.421
Breusch/Godfrey LM (AR/MA1) = 0.437 [0.508]
ARCH test = 0.459 [0.498]
Chow test = 0.588 [0.633]
White het. test = 8.297 [0.141]
Jarque-Bera normality test = 1.218 [0.544]

Imports:
QM = QDEM - Y

2. 3. Government Sector

Regarding existing evidence of tax elasticities with respect to output, Karadeloglou and Koutsouvelis (1991) provided estimates for tax receipts that are characterised by elasticities higher than one. Garganas (1992) provided a detailed system of tax equations that includes direct taxation on various types of personal, corporate and property income, indirect taxes on domestic consumption and imports, and social insurance contributions. The elasticity of tax accruals with respect to personal income (either from employment or other sources) was found to be less than unity, implying that a growth in output is not equiproportionally reflected in higher tax revenues. Moreover, he estimated actual tax receipts in each period as a sum of past accruals to account for the fact that collection delays frequently exceed a year and result in serious revenue losses.

Christodoulakis (1994a) developed a neoclassical model of taxation and arrears accumulation, and, estimating a reduced form equation for total taxes, confirmed the existence of a strong Tanzi-effect (Tanzi, 1978) due to the presence of collection lags in Greece. Given the relatively high rate of inflation in Greece and the absence of indexation in arrears, collection lags eroded the real value of revenues to an extent that exceeded the implicit rise due to fiscal drag.

In the government sector, total revenues consist of direct taxes, indirect taxes, and non-tax revenues generated by various types of state services and fees (such as rent of public buildings, road tolls, etc.). Direct and indirect taxes are functions of output with long-run elasticities of 1.17 and 1.12 respectively. The corresponding short-run elasticities are found to be much lower and equal to 0.87 and 1.08. Changes in non-tax revenues depend on public investment and the output growth rate as an indication of economic activity. Public spending consists of domestic transfer payments, subsidies and transfers abroad.

Direct taxes:
<u>Long-run equation</u>:
logTXD = - 3.968 + 1.169*logGDP
(0.113) (0.015)
Adjusted R-squared = 0.997
Augmented Dickey-Fuller = -4.403 [0.012]

Short-run equation:

$$\Delta logTXD = 0.071 - 0.277*\Delta logTXD(-1) + 1.102*\Delta logGDP - 0.800*Z(-1)$$
$$(0.101)(0.204) \qquad (0.491) \qquad (0.392)$$

Adjusted R-squared = 0.602
Breusch/Godfrey LM (AR/MA1) = 0.197 [0.657]
ARCH test = 0.004 [0.947]
Chow test = 2.018 [0.156]
White het. test = 6.162 [0.724]
Jarque-Bera normality test = 0.629 [0.730]

Indirect taxes:

Long-run equation:

$$logTXI = -2.728 + 1.125*logGDP$$
$$(0.124) \quad (0.015)$$

Adjusted R-squared = 0.996
Augmented Dickey-Fuller = -3.450 [0.074]

Short-run equation:

$$\Delta logTXI = 0.486*\Delta logTXI(-1) + 0.565*\Delta logGDP - 0.803*Z(-1)$$
$$(0.176) \qquad (0.211) \qquad (0.197)$$

Adjusted R-squared = 0.469
Breusch/Godfrey LM (AR/MA1) = 0.155 [0.694]
ARCH test = 0.185 [0.667]
Chow test = 0.867 [0.481]
White het. test = 7.706 [0.564]
Jarque-Bera normality test = 0.272 [0.873]

Non-tax government revenue:

$$\Delta logQYGE = -2.359 + 0.718*logQIG + 4.479*\Delta logQGDP(-1)$$
$$(0.978) \; (0.300) \qquad (1.934)$$

Adjusted R-squared = 0.248
Breusch/Godfrey LM (AR/MA1) = 0.026 [0.872]
ARCH test = 0.129 [0.719]
Chow test = 0.687 [0.576]
White het. test = 8.527 [0.129]
Jarque-Bera normality test = 0.083 [0.959]

Finally, public debt as a ratio to output accumulates by interest payments adjusted for inflation and the growth rate, and by public deficit. Public debt and deficit are postrecursive and used for the implementation of the Convergence Plan.

Public debt as a ratio to output:

$$BY = DY \underset{(1.729)}{-7.674} + ((1+IR12)/((1+\Delta logPGDP)*(1+\Delta logQGDP)))*BY(-1)$$

Adjusted R-squared = 0.961
Durbin' h = 2.124

3. MODEL IDENTITIES

3. 1. Supply And Demand Determination

Supply determination of output:
Y = YTR+YNT+YPS+YAG

Non-agricultural output:
YNA = YTR+YNT+YPS

Demand determination of output (national accounting identity):
QGDP=QCP+QCG+QIP+QIG+QD+QX-QM-QFCA+QSTAT

Per capita growth rate:
RPC = 100*((Y/POP)/(Y(-1)/POP(-1))-1)

Labour productivity growth:
RTR = 100*((Y/L)/(Y(-1)/L(-1))-1)

Total spending:
QSP = QCP+QCG+QIP+QIG+QD+QSTAT

Total demand:
QDEM=QCP+QCG+QIP+QIG+QD+QX-QFCA+QSTAT

Nominal GDP:
GDP=QGDP*PGDP

3. 2. Wage Rate And Unit Labour Cost

Average wage rate:
WR = ((WMFH*8*22)*LTR+WTRD*LNT)/(LTR+LNT)

Real wage rate:
QWR = WR/PGDP

Nominal unit labour cost:
ΔlogULC = Δlog(WR)-Δlog(Y/L)

Wage bill in the public sector:
WPUB = WPS*LPS

3. 3. Investment

Private investment:
QIP = QITR+QINT

3. 4. Interest Rates And The Cost Of Capital

12-month interest rate:
IR12 = RIR12+INFY

Real price of capital in tradable sector:
RPKTR=(PIP/PGDP)*(IRLC+10.0-100*Δlog(PIP))

Real price of capital in non-tradable sector:
RPKNT=(PIP/PGDP)*(IRTRD+10.0-100*Δlog(PIP))

Short-term interest rate:
IRSH = IRSH(-1)+(IR12-IR12(-1))

Long-term interest rate:
IRLC = IRLC(-1)+IR12-IR12(-1)

Interest rate in trade:
IRTRD = IRTRD(-1)+IR12-IR12(-1)

Interest rate in agriculture:
IRAG = IRAG(-1)+IR12-IR12(-1)

3. 5. Labour

Non-agricultural employment:
LNA = LTR+LNT+LPS

Total employment:
L = LNA+LAGR

Participation rate:
$\Delta\log(LFNAU/POP) = 0.08 * \Delta\log(WR/PGDP)$

Urban employment:
$\Delta\log(LNAU) = 0.75 * \Delta\log(LNA)$

Number of urban unemployed:
UUL = LFNAU-LNAU

Urban unemployment rate:
UUR = 100*UUL/LFNAU

3. 6. Deflators And Inflation Rates

GDP deflator:
PGDP=(PTR*YTR+PNT*YNT+PPS*YPS+PYA*YAG)
/(YTR+YNT+YPS+YAG)

CPI inflation:
INFC = 100*(CPI/CPI(-1)-1)

WPI inflation:
INFW = 100*(WPI/WPI(-1)-1)

GDP inflation:
INFY = 100*(PGDP/PGDP(-1)-1)

Price of imports:
$\Delta\log(PM) = \Delta\log(WCPI*XED)$

3. 7. Government Sector

Subsidies:
SUB = QSUB*PGDP

Transfers to private sector:
TRD = QTRD*PGDP

Transfers in the rest of the world:
TRF = QTRF*PGDP

Non-tax government revenue in current prices:
YGE = QYGE*PGDP

Factor cost adjustment:
$\Delta\log FCA = \Delta\log TXI$

Public deficit:
DEF = QCG*PCG + QIG*PIG – TXD – TXI + SUB + TRD + TRF – YGE – REEC*XECU

Public deficit as percentage of GDP:
DY = 100*DEF/(Y*PGDP)

Direct tax rate:
RTD = 100*TXD/(Y*PGDP)

3. 8. Foreign Sector

Trade deficit:
TDEF = (QM*PM) - (QX*PX)

Trade deficit as GDP percentage
JY = 100*TDEF/(Y*PGDP)

Terms of trade:
TTR = 100*PX/PM

Exchange rates:

XED = XED(-1) *(XECU/XECU(-1))

4. MODELLING ENERGY DEMAND

4.1. Sectoral Energy Demand

Energy demand in the tradable sector:

Long-run equation:

logETR=4.868 + 0.762*logYTR(-1) - 0.194*log[PETR(-1)/PTR(-1)]
(0.744) (0.169) (0.067)

Adjusted R-squared = 0.494
Augmented Dickey-Fuller = -2.608 [0.280]

Short-run equation:

ΔlogETR=0.001 + 0.797*ΔlogYTR(-1) - 0.253*Δlog[PETR(-1)/PTR(-1)]
(0.010)(0.300) (0.098)
-0.441*Z(-1)
(0.239)

Adjusted R-squared = 0.383
Breusch/Godfrey LM (AR/MA1) = 0.468 [0.494]
ARCH test = 0.123 [0.726]
Chow test = 1.121 [0.395]
White het. test = 5.801 [0.760]
Jarque-Bera normality test = 1.274 [0.529]

Energy demand in the non-tradable sector:

Long-run equation:

logENT1 = 0.537 + 1.512*logYNT(-1) - 0.240*log(PENT/PNT)
(0.246) (0.046) (0.077)

Adjusted R-squared = 0.982
Augmented Dickey-Fuller = -3.118 [0.130]

Short-run equation:

$$\Delta logENT1 = \underset{(0.017)}{0.009} + \underset{(0.518)}{1.270}*\Delta logYNT(-1) - \underset{(0.095)}{0.226}*\Delta log(PENT/PNT) \underset{(0.277)}{-0.691}*Z(-1)$$

Adjusted R-squared = 0.333
Breusch/Godfrey LM (AR/MA1) = 0.587 [0.444]
ARCH test = 0.356 [0.551]
Chow test = 1.521 [0.263]
White het. test = 6.739 [0.664]
Jarque-Bera normality test = 1.280 [0.527]

Aggregate energy demand in the public and agricultural sectors:

Long-run equation:

$$logENT2 = \underset{(0.689)}{-1.636} + \underset{(0.138)}{1.955}*log(YPS(-1)+YAG(-1))$$

Adjusted R-squared = 0.912
Augmented Dickey-Fuller = -5.187 [0.003]

Short-run equation:

$$\Delta logENT2 = \underset{(0.009)}{0.026} + \underset{(0.257)}{0.637}*\Delta log(YPS+YAG) - \underset{(0.141)}{0.343}*Z(-1)$$

Adjusted R-squared = 0.451
Breusch/Godfrey LM (AR/MA1) = 0.011 [0.915]
ARCH test = 0.014 [0.906]
Chow test = 0.645 [0.599]
White het. test = 5.566 [0.351]
Jarque-Bera normality test = 0.220 [0.896]

4.2. Demand By Type Of Energy

Demand for oil:

Long-run equation:

$$LogOIL = \underset{(0.397)}{3.106} + \underset{(0.065)}{0.997}*logY(-1) - \underset{(0.063)}{0.220}*log[POIL(-1)/PGDP(-1)]$$

Adjusted R-squared = 0.927
Augmented Dickey-Fuller = -3.722 [0.046]

<u>Short-run equation:</u>

$$\Delta \log OIL = \underset{(0.011)}{0.010} + \underset{(0.341)}{0.785}*\Delta \log Y - \underset{(0.073)}{0.161}*\Delta \log[POIL(-1)/PGDP(-1)] \underset{(0.213)}{-0.516}*Z(-1)$$

Adjusted R-squared = 0.406
Breusch/Godfrey LM (AR/MA1) = 0.002 [0.965]
ARCH test = 0.220 [0.639]
Chow test = 1.249 [0.347]
White het. test = 10.0 [0.347]
Jarque-Bera normality test = 0.986 [0.611]

Demand for electricity:

<u>Long-run equation</u>:

$$\log ELE = \underset{(0.471)}{-3.053} + \underset{(0.078)}{1.758}*\log Y$$

Adjusted R-squared = 0.964
Augmented Dickey-Fuller = -2.932 [0.175]

<u>Short-run equation</u>:

$$\Delta \log ELE = \underset{(0.009)}{0.019} + \underset{(0.283)}{1.121}*\Delta \log Y \underset{(0.107)}{-0.141}*\Delta \log(PELE/PGDP) \underset{(0.148)}{-0.234}*Z(-1)$$

Adjusted R-squared = 0.524
Breusch/Godfrey LM (AR/MA1) = 1.371 [0.242]
ARCH test = 2,578 [0.108]
Chow test = 1.562 [0.252]
White het. test = 6.831 [0.655]
Jarque-Bera normality test = 0.726 [0.695]

4.3. Energy Prices And Price Linkages

Price of oil:

$$\Delta \log[POIL/(1+VAT)] = \underset{(0.030)}{-0.018} + \underset{(0.170)}{0.600}*\Delta \log ULC + (1-0.600)*\Delta \log(XED*POILF)$$

Adjusted R-squared = 0.144
DW-statistic = 1.712

Price of electricity:

$$\Delta logPELE = 0.002 + 0.959*\Delta logULC + (1-0.959)*\Delta log(XED*POILF)$$
(0.020) (0.078)

Adjusted R-squared = 0.130
DW-statistic = 1.466

Price of energy in the tradable sector:

$$\Delta logPETR = 0.442*\Delta logPOIL + 0.400*\Delta logPELE + (1-0.442-0.400) *\Delta logPSOL$$
(0.132) (0.146)

Adjusted R-squared = 0.917
DW-statistic = 0.947

Price of energy in the non-tradable sector:

$$\Delta logPENT = 0.759*\Delta logPOIL + (1-0.759)*\Delta logPELE(-1)$$
(0.091)

Adjusted R-squared = 0.9390
DW-statistic = 1.236

Wholesale price index:

$$\Delta logWPI = -0.002 + 0.553*\Delta logULC + 0.178*\Delta logPM + (1-0.553-0.178)*\Delta logPE$$
(0.008) (0.114) (0.152)

Adjusted R-squared = 0.685
DW-statistic = 1.670

Tradable sector output deflator:

$$\Delta logPTR = 0.578*\Delta logULC + 0.288*\Delta logPM + (1-0.578-0.288)*\Delta logPE$$
(0.137) (0.183)

Adjusted R-squared = 0.480
DW-statistic = 1.544

Non-tradable sector output deflator:

$$\Delta \log PNT = -0.008 + 0.840{*}\Delta \log ULC + (1-0.840){*}\Delta \log PE$$
$$\qquad (0.008)\ (0.078)$$

Adjusted R-squared = 0.312
DW-statistic = 1.525

4.5. Energy Model Identities

Demand for solid fuel:

SOL = (ETR+ENT1+ENT2) - OIL - ELE

Total price of energy:

PE = OIL/(OIL+ELE+SOL)*POIL+ELE/(OIL+ELE+SOL)*PELE+
SOL/(OIL+ELE+SOL)*PSOL

LIST OF VARIABLES

Name	Description	Type	Source
BY	Public dept-to-output ratio, percent	E	trf.
CPI	Consumer price index, 1970=1	E	ESYE
DEF	Public deficit	I	trf.
DY	Public deficit-to-output ratio, percent	I	trf.
D80	Dummy variable for year 1980	D	trf.
D82	Dummy variable for year 1982	D	trf.
ETR	Energy demand by the tradable sector	E	trf.
ENT1	Energy demand by the non-tradable sector	E	trf.
ENT2	Energy demand by the public-agricultural sectors	E	trf.
ELE	Electricity demand	E	trf.
FCA	Factor cost adjustment	I	trf.
GDP	Gross domestic product at factor cost, GDR bn	I	BG
INFC	Inflation rate, consumer price index, percent	I	trf.
INFW	Inflation rate, wholesale price index, percent	I	trf.
INFY	GDP inflation rate, percent	I	trf.
IRAG	Long-term interest rate for agriculture, percent	I	BG
IRLC	Long-term interest rate for the industry, percent	I	BG
IRSH	Short-term interest rate for the industry, percent	I	BG
IRTRD	Interest rate for trade, percent	I	BG
IR12	Treasury Bill rate, 12-month, percent	I	BG
JY	Trade deficit to output ratio, percent	I	trf.
L	Total employment, thousands	I	ESYE
LAGR	Employment in agriculture, thousands	E	ESYE
LFNAU	Urban labour force, thousands	E	ESYE
LNA	Non-agricultural employment, thousands	I	trf.
LNAU	Urban non-agricultural labour, thousands	E	ESYE
LNT	Employment in non-tradable sector, thousands	E	trf.
LPS	Employment in public sector, thousands	X	trf.
LTR	Employment in tradable sector, thousands	E	trf.
PCG	Public consumption deflator, 1970=1	E	ESYE
PE	Weighted energy price index	I	trf.
PELE	Price of electricity, 1970=1	E	trf.
PETR	Price of energy in the tradable sector, 1970=1	E	trf.

PENT	Price of energy in the non-tradable sector, 1970=1	E	trf.
PGDP	GDP deflator, 1970=1	I	trf.
PIG	Public investment deflator, 1970=1	E	ESYE
PIP	Private investment deflator, 1970=1	E	trf.
PM	Imports deflator, 1970=1	E	CEC
PNT	Non-tradable sector price deflator, 1970=1	E	trf.
POIL	Price of oil, 1970=1	E	trf.
POILF	Average annual price of oil (USD per barrel)	X	IFS
POP	Population, thousands	X	ESYE
PPS	Public sector price deflator, 1970=1	E	trf.
PSOL	Price of solid fuel, 1970=1	X	trf.
PTR	Tradable sector price deflator, 170=1	E	trf.
PX	Exports deflator, 1970=1	E	CEC
PYA	Agricultural product deflator, 1970=1	E	trf.
QCG	Public consumption, 1970 GDR bn	E	ESYE
QCP	Private consumption, 1970 GDR bn	E	BG
QD	Change in inventories, 1970 GDR bn	E	ESYE
QDEM	Total demand, 1970 GDR bn	I	trf.
QFCA	Factor cost adjustment, 1970 GDR bn	E	trf.
QFWP	Private financial wealth, real, 1970 GDR bn	E	trf.
QGDP	Gross domestic product at factor cost, 1970 GDR bn	I	ESYE
QIA	Agricultural investment, 1970 GDR bn	E	ESYE
QIG	Public investment, 1970 GDR bn	X	ESYE
QINT	Investment in non-tradable sector, 1970 GDR bn	E	ESYE
OIL	Oil demand	E	trf.
QIP	Private investment, 1970 GDR bn	E	BG
QITR	Investment in tradable sector, 1970 GDR bn	E	ESYE
QKA	Agricultural capital stock, 1970 GDR bn	E	KEPE
QKG	Public capital stock, 1970 GDR bn	E	KEPE
QKP	Private capital stock, 1970 GDR bn	E	KEPE
QM	Imports of goods and services, 1970 GDR bn	I	CEC
QSP	Total gross domestic expenditure, 1970 GDR bn	I	ESYE
QSTAT	Statistical differences, 1970 GDR bn	X	ESYE
QSUB	Subsidies, real, 1970 GDR bn	X	ESYE
QTRD	Transfers to private sector, real	X	trf.
QTRF	Transfers abroad, real	X	trf.
QWR	Average wage rate, real	I	trf.
QX	Exports of goods and services, 1970 GDR bn	E	CEC
QYGE	Non-tax government income, 1970 GDR bn	E	trf.

REEC	Net receipts from EU, ECU mn	X	BG
RIR12	Real interest rate, 12-month	X	trf.
RPC	GDP per capita growth rate	I	trf.
RPKNT	Real price of capital in non-tradable sector	I	trf.
RPKTR	Real price of capital in tradable sector	I	trf.
RTD	Direct tax rate	I	trf.
RTR	Labour productivity growth	I	trf.
SUB	Subsidies to private sector, GDR bn	I	ESYE
TDEF	Trade deficit	I	trf.
TRD	Net transfers to households and enterprises, GDR bn	I	ESYE
TRF	Current transfers abroad, GDR bn	I	ESYE
TTR	Terms of trade, 1970=100	I	trf.
TXD	Direct taxes, total, GDR bn	I	BG
TXI	Indirect taxes, total, GDR bn	E	BG
T74	Linear trend starting at year 1974	D	trf.
ULC	Nominal unit labour cost, 1970=1	I	CEC
ULCEC	Nominal unit labour cost in EUR15, 1970=1	X	CEC
UUL	Number of urban unemployed, thousands	I	BG
UUR	Urban unemployment rate	I	BG
VAT	Average VAT rate	I	trf.
WCPI	OECD consumer price index, total, 1970=1	X	OECD
WGDP	OECD gross domestic product, 1985 USD bn	X	OECD
WMFH	Hourly compensation of workers in industry	E	BG
WPI	Wholesale price Index, 1970=1	E	BG
WPS	Wage rate in the public sector	E	trf.
WPUB	Wage bill in the public sector	I	BG
WR	Average wage rate in non-agriculture, GDR	I	trf.
WTRD	Monthly compensation of employees in trade	E	BG
XECU	Drachma/ECU exchange rate	E	BG
XED	Drachma/Dollar exchange rate	I	BG
Y	Total output, 1970 GDR bn	I	BG
YAG	Agricultural output, 1970 GDR bn	E	ESYE
YGE	Non-tax government income, GDR bn	I	ESYE
YNA	Non-agricultural output, 1970 GDR bn	I	trf.
YNT	Output of non-tradable sector, 1970 GDR bn	E	ESYE
YPS	Output of public sector, 1970 GDR bn	E	ESYE
YTR	Output of tradable sector, 1970 GDR bn	E	ESYE

Note: E denotes endogenous variable, X denotes exogenous variable, I denotes identity and D denotes definition.

DATA SOURCES

1. National Accounts, various editions by the National Statistical Service (ESYE).
2. Price bulletins, various editions by ESYE.
3. Monthly statistical bulletin, Bank of Greece (BG).
4. Centre for Economic Planning (KEPE).
5. European Economy, various editions by the Commission of the European Communities (CEC).
6. OECD, Main Economic Indicators (OECD).
7. International Financial Statistics, IMF (IFS).
8. Variables indicated by 'trf.' are obtained by transforming original data.

ENDNOTES

[1] See, for example, Aschauer (1989).

[2] Deno (1988).

[3] As noted by Holtz-Eakin (1994) this distinction is in principle important, although in practice it appears to have a limited effect in the empirical assessment of the role of public capital.

[4] Today, it is widely acknowledged that the monitoring and control of regional expenditure was inadequate, and, therefore, a major reform was needed. The EU, in an effort to improve the co-ordination and effectiveness of Structural Funds, pushed for a substantial revision in 1993, in accordance to Article 2 of the Maastricht Treaty. For an analytical description of these events, see Bachtler and Michie (1994, 1995).

[5] Moreover, in 1985 the Integrated Mediterranean Programmes (IMP) were introduced as compensation to Greece, Italy and France for the entrance of Spain and Portugal in the Community. These resources were supplementary to those received through Structural Funds and, practically, '..it is impossible to isolate to what extent the post 1986 increases can be attributed to the IMP' (Plaskovitis, 1994).

[6] See Bradley et al. (1995b) for an extensive treatment of the first CSF and the specific features for each of the four recipient countries (Greece, Ireland, Portugal and Spain).

[7] Synoptic Presentation of Priority Axes of the CSF 1994-99 (Ministry of National Economy, 1994).

[8] Moreover, as pointed out by Granger (1986), a large data span is far more important than the number of observations for the cointegration testing procedure. In this sense, a period of 21 years should be adequate to reveal the links between the variables under consideration.

[9] During the early eighties wage increases followed past price increases, thus contributing to inflation acceleration and the rise of nominal and real unit labour cost. In 1985 a wage freeze was imposed as part of the stabilisation package imposed. During the last years, an attempt is made to establish long-term collective labor agreements linked to productivity and expected inflation targets (the latter being determined by the Convergence Programme).

[10] This figure is the estimated value for the period 1982-1994 for which reliable data on the labour force exist.

[11] The base forecast does not take into account the implementation of CSF and its impact on the economy, and so any comparison with realized outcomes of the variables should give a measure of the effects brought about by the actual CSF intervention; see chapter 4.

[12] By assumption, real interest rates are kept constant and primary surpluses have to meet the same prescribed targets as in the baserun.

[13] When the built-in deficit stabilization rule operates the results are similar, except for the public debt to output ratio which improves slightly due to the initial rise of output.

[14] However, in their work the corresponding infrastructure supply-side effects in the form

of externalities are not enabled.

[15] In a similar vein, Bradley et al. (1995a) adopt *ad hoc* the values 5% for Ireland, 10% for Portugal and 20% for Spain.

[16] Some evidence on the effects of activities such as educational facilities and public services is provided by Aschauer (1989). These factors are found to have a significantly positive impact on productivity which, however, is smaller than the corresponding one of hard infrastructure. This could be attributed to the substantial number of lags that one would expect for e.g. educational buildings on productivity. Also, a number of other indirect positive effects should be underlined, such as the increase in life expectancy due to improved health infrastructure and services (particularly when accompanied by better work habits and a higher level of skills); see also Barro and Sala-I-Martin (1995, chapter 12).

[17] According to the 1991 census, the number of secondary education graduates in Greece is roughly 1.8 mn persons, while the total workforce consists of 3.9 mn persons.

[18] See Mamuneas and Savvides (1999). It is noteworthy that this estimate allows the calculation of the *social rate of return for human capital* in Greece, namely the additional units of output per worker gained (or lost) as a result of a unitary increase in human capital (proxied by years of schooling) relative to the opportunity cost of schooling (proxied by the real wage rate of unskilled labour). Estimates for Greece by the same authors show that the social rate of return (0.057) is higher than the corresponding private rate of return (0.027); this, according to the Lucas (1988) model, implies the presence of nonnegative externalities for human capital accumulation in Greece and that, consequently, education should be publicly financed.

[19] The human capital model (Becker, 1975) predicts that the stock of human capital rises with experience, resulting in lower *initial wages* but in a rising *wage profile* for human capital investors; this pattern is confirmed by empirical studies for the U.S. (see Neumark and Taubman, 1995).

[20] To evaluate the effects of CSF on the public deficit and, simultaneously, maintain the fiscal stabilization hypothesis, we assume that public debt as a ratio to output remains fixed at the base level, while public deficit adjusts every period to achieve this pre-specified level. So, public deficit increases during the period of implementation to finance the extra needs of public contribution, but returns to the baserun level thereafter.

[21] The implementation of CSF in these models involves a 'CSF-type' shock with annualized amounts calculated as GDP percent for every country. The shock is assumed to affect the economy in five stages, ranging for the 'no supply-side effects' case to the 'full supply-side effects'scenario. The shock is sustained unchanged after the ending of the Program under the same -arbitrary- cofinancing arrangement (1:1) for all countries. the numerical effects of output are heavily dependent on the hypothesized values of the supply-side effects for each country. Unfortunately, no results for the consequences of the 'CSF type' shock on the rest of the variables in these economies are reported. On the contrary, the simulation results for the Greek economy are based on the realized CSF investment or on official projections, and take place under the hypothesis that the capital inflow from abroad will terminate with the end of the CSF.

[22] Note that a rigorous evaluation of the employment effects of CSF would require the estimation from microeconomic studies of the 'windfall' effect (benefits which would have been secured in the absence of EU funding) and the 'displacement' effect (effects in employment which result in job movements from other areas covered by the Programme).

Also, under the present macromodelling setting no distinction can be made between jobs maintained or altered (i.e. those that would be lost in the absence of assistance) and jobs arising from assistance (see European Commission, 1997b).

[23] Ikonomikos Tachydromos (23 October 1997, p. 17). According to the same source, the lowest rates are observed in the educational and unemployment programs, where only 16% of total planned inflows have been absorbed.

[24] A detailed description of the energy features in Greece can be found in a study by KEPE (1991).

[25] The oil price considered here was taken as the average crude price derived from spot crude oil prices for Dubai, UK Brent and Alaskan N. Slope reserves, which correspond to equal consumption of medium light and heavy oil on a worldwide scale.

[26] A dummy is included for the year 1986 in the price of oil equation when the international price of oil fell by 60%, but the fall was not allowed to puss over domestic prices.

[27] Note that the price of solid fuel is considered exogenous because solid fuel is determined residually and, therefore, its price does not affect directly the rest of the energy demand system.

[28] Since data for non-fuel import prices is not available, a rise in foreign fuel (oil) prices operates through two channels: first, by raising the price of imports, and, second, by increasing the domestic price of oil.

[29] These discrepancies are well within the uncertainty range of the actual data collection system and are expressed as 'statistical differences' in Annual Energy Balances.

[30] An alternative solution involves a carbon tax, i.e. an energy tax directly proportional to the carbon content of the fuel. Proost and Van Regemorter (1992) show that this type of taxation is more efficient in achieving the desired CO_2 emission target through the reduction of carbon intensive fuel.

[31] This section draws upon Christodoulakis et al. (2000).

[32] Approximately 85% of this total will be imported from Russia, via Bulgaria, by pipeline and the remaining 15% will be imported from Algeria in liquefied form. The construction of the main transmission pipeline was completed in July 1995, while the construction of secondary pipelines is progressing. The supply of natural gas to the first Public Power Corporation (PPC) gas-fired power station began in 1997, while two more power stations in South Attica are scheduled to come on-line by the end of 1998. Furthermore, another natural gas fired station in Northern Greece is expected to come on-line by the end of 2001. According to the specified timetable, it is estimated that the PPC will be in a position to absorb approximately 1.1 billion Nm^3 of natural gas by the year 2000 and 1.5 billion Nm^3 by the year 2001.

[33] In the industrial sector, PGC has already formulated a pricing policy and the general terms of gas supply to industrial customers, and is aggressively pursuing contracts with industrial customers. Nine contracts have already been signed for sale of more than 0.3 billion Nm^3/yr and a few large industrial units are already connected to the distribution network, while negotiations with other industries are in progress. City networks are presently under construction and will be completed by the year 2000.

[34] The terms Oil and Coal cover all petroleum products and solid fuels, respectively, used in the three sectors of the economy, except for the amounts used for electricity generation. The emission factors have been derived by considering both total emissions and total final

consumption from the tradable, non-tradable and public and tertiary sectors according to estimates provided in the Greek *National Inventory of Greenhouse and Other Gases for the years 1990-1995.*

[35] See *Climate Change: The Greek Action Plan for the Abatement of CO_2 and Other Greenhouse Gas Emissions* (1995), and *2nd National Communication to the UNFCCC* (1997).

[36] The European Council also agreed that the maximum co-financing ratio should be set to 75% of total cost and, in general, should be above 50% for national expenditure schemes eligible under Objective 1.

REFERENCES

Alogoskoufis G., 1990, 'Competitiveness, wage adjustment and macroeconomic policy in the dependent economy: The case of Greece', *Greek Economic Review,* 12, 15-57.

Alogoskoufis G., 1995, 'The two faces of Janus: Institutions, policy regimes and macroeconomic performance in Greece', *Economic Policy*, April, 149-192.

Anton V., A. De Bustos, J.A. Herce and S. Sosvilla-Rivero, 1999, 'Environmental consequences of the Community Support Framework 1994-1999 in Spain', *Journal of Policy Modeling*, 21, 831-850.

Argimon I., J.M. Gonzalez-Paramo, M.J. Martin and J.M. Roldan (1993), 'Productivity and infrastructure in the Spanish economy', *Banco de Espana Working Paper*, No.9313.

Arrow K. J., H. B. Chenery, B. S. Minhas and R. M. Solow, 1961, 'Capital-labour substitution and economic efficiency', *Review of Economics and Statistics*, 43, 225-250.

Arrow K. and M. Kurz, 1970, *Public Investment, the Rate of Return and Optimal Fiscal Policy*, John Hopkins Press, Baltimore.

Aschauer D. A., 1989, 'Is public expenditure productive?', *Journal of Monetary Economics*, 23, 177-200.

Bacthler J. and R. Michie, 1994, 'Strengthening economic and social cohesion? The revision of the Structural Funds', *Regional Studies*, 28, 789-796.

Bacthler J. and R. Michie, 1995, 'A new era in EU regional policy evaluation? The appraisal of the Structural Funds', *Regional Studies*, 29, 745-751.

Bajo-Rubio O. and S. Sosvilla-Rivero, 1993, 'Does public capital affect private sector performance?', *Economic Modelling*, 10, 3, 179-185.

Banerjee A., J. Dolado, J.W. Galbraith and D.F. Hendry, 1993, *Co-Integration, Error-correction, and the Analysis of Non-stationary Data,* Oxford University Press, New York.

Barro R.J. and J. Lee, 1994, 'Sources of economic growth', *Carnegie-Rochester Conference Series on Public Policy*, 40, 1-46.

Barro R.J. and X. Sala-i-Martin, 1995, *Economic Growth*, MIT Press, Cambridge.

Becker G., 1975, *Human Capital: A Theoretical and Empirical Analysis*, 2nd edition, The University of Chicago Press, Chicago.

Beutel J., 1996, 'Dynamic input-output model to evaluate the economic impact of the Structural Funds', *paper presented at the European Conference on evaluation methods for Structural Funds intervention.*

Bradley J., J. A. Herce and L. Modesto, 1995a, 'The macroeconomic effects of the CSF 1994-99 in the EU periphery: An analysis based on the HERMIN Model', *Economic Modelling*, 12, 3, 323-333.

Bradley J., N. O'Donell, N. Sheridan and K. Whelan, 1995b, *Regional Aid and Convergence*, Avebury.

Bradley J., K. Whelan and J. Wright, 1995c, 'HERMIN Ireland', *Economic Modelling*, 12, 3, 249-274.

Brennan P., 1993, 'The impact of CSF 1989-93', *Confederation of European Industries*, Brussels.

Capros P. and P. Karadeloglou, 1989, 'Macroeconomic Impacts of Structural Funds on the Greek Economy', *Institute of Economic and Industrial Research.*

Capros P., P. Karadeloglou and G. Mentzas, 1988, 'Structure and properties of the GEM-NTUA macroeconomic model for Greece', *Discussion Paper, National Technical University of Athens.*

Caramanis M. C., 1981, 'Elasticity of substitution between capital and disaggregated labor: A cost function application with Greek data on the level of the firm', *Greek Economic Review*, 3, 187-196.

Christodoulakis N., 1994a, 'Tax-collection lags and the revenue maximising inflation', *Empirical Economics*, 19, 329-342.

Christodoulakis N., 1994b, 'Fiscal developments in Greece and the scope for budget consolidation', *European Economy*, 3, 97-134.

Christodoulakis N., S. P. Dimelis and T. Kollintzas, 1995, 'Comparisons of business cycles in the EC: Idiosyncrasies and regularities', *Economica*, 62, 1-27.

Christodoulakis N., S. Kalyvitis, D. Lalas and S. Pesmajoglou, 2000, 'Forecasting energy consumption and energy related CO_2 emissions in Greece', *Energy Economics*, 22, 4, 395-423.

Christodoulakis N. and I. Segoura, 1994, 'Inadequate Infrastructure and rising cost: The decline of Greek manufacturing', *AUEB Discussion Paper*, No. 94-01.

Climate Change: The Greek Action Plan for the Abatement of CO_2 and Other Greenhouse Gas Emissions, Athens, 1995, Ministry for the Environment, Physical Planning and Public Works / National Technical University of Athens, Athens.

CSF: A synopsis of development axes for Greece, 1994, *Ministry of National Economy*, July, (in greek).

Devarajan S. and V. Swaroop, 1998, 'The implications of foreign aid fungibility for development assistance', *World Bank Working Paper*, No. 2022.

Dimeli, S., T. Kollintzas and N.M. Christodoulakis, 1997, *Economic Fluctuations and Development in Greece and Europe*, IMOP Editions, Athens (in greek).

European Commission, 1996, *Energy in Europe (European Energy to 2020: A Scenario Approach)*, DG XVII, Brussels.

European Commission, 1997a, *The Impact of Structural Policies on Economic and Social Cohesion in the Union 1989-99*, Regional Development Studies No. 26, Brussels.

European Commission, 1997b, *9th Annual Report of the Structural Funds*, DG XVI, Brussels.

European Commission, 1999, *Sixth Periodic Report on the Social and Economic Situation and Development of the Regions of the European Union*, DG XVI, Brussels.

Engle R. and C. Granger, 1987, 'Co-integration and error correction: representation, estimation and testing', *Econometrica*, 55, 251-276.

Ford R. and P. Poret, 1991, 'Infrastructure and private sector productivity', *OECD Economic Studies*, 16, 79-131.

Garganas N., 1992, *The Bank of Greece Econometric Model of the Greek economy,* Bank of Greece, Athens.

Gaspar V. and A.M. Pereira, 1995, 'The impact of financial integration and unilateral public transfers on investment and growth in EC capital-importing countries', *Journal of Development Economies*, 48, 43-66.

Georgoutsos D., 1992, 'Dynamic factor demands under imperfect competition: the Greek manufacturing industry 1958-81', *Applied Economics*, 24, 1009-1015.

Granger C., 1986, 'Developments in the study of co-integrated economic variables', *Oxford Bulletin of Economics and Statistics*, 48, 3, 213-228.

Halikias J., 1988, 'The determination of Greek exports: A disaggregated model', *Rivista*

Internazionale di Scienze Economiche e Commerciali, 35, 473-486.
Hall R. and C. Jones, 1999, 'Why do some countries produce so much more output per worker than others', *Quarterly Journal of Economics*, 114, 1, 83-116.
Herce J. A. and S. Sosvilla-Rivero, 1995, 'HERMIN Spain', *Economic Modelling*, 12, 3, 295-311.
Holtz-Eakin D., 1994, 'Public-sector capital and the productivity puzzle', *Review of Economics and Statistics*, 76, 1, 12-21.
Holtz-Eakin D. and T.M. Selden, 1995, 'Stoking the fires? CO_2 emissions and economic growth', *Journal of Public Economics*, 57, 85-101.
Ioannides Y. M. and M. C. Caramanis, 1979, 'Capital-labor substitution in a developing country: The case of Greece - A note', *European Economic Review*, 12, 101-110.
Karadeloglou P., 1992, 'Energy tax versus carbon tax: A quantitative macroeconomic analysis with the Hermes/Midas model', *European Economy*, Special edition, No. 1, 153-184.
Karadeloglou P. and P. Koutsouvelis, 1991, 'Macroeconometric model KEPE-LINK (MYKL)', *Centre of Planning and Economic Research Studies*, No. 5, Athens.
KEPE, 1991, *Reports on the 1988-1992 Program: Energy*, KEPE editions, Athens (in greek).
Kintis A., 1977, 'Capital-labour substitution in a developing country: The case of Greece-Comments and some new results', *European Economic Review*, 9, 379-382.
Kollias C. and S. Makrydakis, 1995, 'The causal relationship between tax revenues and government spending in Greece: 1950-1990', *Cyprus Journal of Economics*, 8, 120-135.
Kotlikoff, L. and J. Gokhale, 1992, 'Estimating a firm's age-productivity profile using the present value of workers' earnings', *Quarterly Journal of Economics*, 107, 4, 1215-42.
Koutsouvelis P. and J. Anastassakou, 1989, 'The Hermes-Greece model', mimeo, *Centre of Planning and Economic Research*, Athens.
Lianos T. P., 1975, 'Capital-labour substitution in a developing country: The case of Greece', *European Economic Review*, 6, 129-141.
Lianos T. P., 1976, 'Factor augmentation in Greek manufacturing', *European Economic Review*, 8, 15-31.
Lolos S. and N. Zonzilos, 1992, 'Evaluation of the economic impact of the CSF on the Greek economy', *Report for the European Commission*, Brussels.
Lolos S., A. Suwa-Eisenmann, N. Zonzilos and F. Bourguignon, 1995, 'Evaluating the CSF with an extended computable general equilibrium model: The case of Greece (1988-1995)', *Journal of Policy Modelling*, 17, 2, 177-197.
Lucas R. E., 1988, 'On the mechanics of economic development', *Journal of Monetary Economics*, 22, 3-42.
Mamatzakis E., 1999, 'Testing for long run relationship between infrastructure and private capital productivity: A time series analysis for the Greek industry', *Applied Economics Letters*, April.
Mamuneas T. and A. Savvides, 1999, 'Economic development and the return to human capital', *University of Cyprus Working Paper*.
Meade J., 1952, 'External economies and diseconomies in a competitive situation', *Economic Journal*, 62, March, 54-67.
Modesto L. and P. D. Neves, 1995, 'HERMIN Portugal', *Economic Modelling*, 12, 3, 275-294.
Munnell A., 1992, 'Infrastructure investment and economic growth', *Journal of Economic*

Perspectives, 6, 4, 189-198.
2nd National Communication to the United Nations Framework Convention on Climate Change, 1997, Ministry for the Environment, Physical Planning and Public Works / National Observatory of Athens, Athens.
National Inventory of Greenhouse and Other Gases for the years 1990-95, 1997, Ministry for the Environment, Physical Planning and Public Works / National Observatory of Athens, Athens.
Neumark, D. and P. Taubman, 1995, 'Why do wage profiles slope upwards? Tests of the general human capital model', *Journal of Labor Economics*, 13, 4, 736-61.
Otto G. and G. M. Voss, 1994, 'Public capital and private sector productivity', *The Economic Record*, 70, 209, 121-132.
Papatheodorou Y., 1991, 'Production structure and cyclical behaviour: Modelling the supply block of the Greek economy', *European Economic Review*, 35, 1449-71.
Patsouratis V. and I. Souflis, 1995, *The effects on the Greek Economy-manufacturing from an Energy-environmental tax*, Contemporary Studies No. 9, Foundation of Industrial and Economic Research, Athens (in greek).
Pereira A.M., 1997, 'Development policies in the EU: An international comparison', *Review of Development Economies*, 1, 219-235.
Pereira A.M., 1999, 'International public transfers and convergence in the European Union', *Public Finance Review*, 27, 194-219.
Plaskovitis I., 1994, 'EC regional policy in Greece: Ten years of Structural Funds intervention', in P. Kazakos and P.C. Ioakimidis (eds.), *Greece and EC Membership Evaluated*, St. Martin's Press, New York.
PNGC, 1997, Progress of the works for the introduction of natural gas in Greece, Public Natural Gas Coorporation, (in greek).
Pfaehler W., U. Hofmann and W. Boente, 1996, 'Does extra public infrastructure capital matter? An appraisal of empirical literature', *Finanzarchiv*, 53, 68-112.
Proost S. and D. Van Regemorter, 1992, 'Carbon taxes in the European Community: Design of tax policies and their welfare impacts', *European Economy*, Special edition No. 1, 91-124.
Provopoulos G. A. and T. Zambaras, 1991, 'Testing the causality between government spending and taxation', *Public Choice*, 68, 277-282.
Ratner J., 1983, 'Government capital and the production function for US private output', *Economic Letters*, 13, 213-217.
Sakellariou C. and D. Juliet Howland, 1993, 'An expenditure determined macroeconometric model of Greece', *Economic Modelling*, 10, 1, 35-56.
Spanos A., 1986, *Statistical Foundations of Econometric Modelling*, Cambridge University Press, Cambridge.
Standaert S., 1992, 'The macro-sectoral effects of an EC-wide energy tax: simulation experiments for 1993-2005', *European Economy*, Special edition, No 1, 127-152.
Surrey J., 1992, 'Energy policy in the European Community: Conflicts between the objectives of the unified single market, supply security and a clean environment', *Energy Journal*, 13, 3, 207-231.
Tanzi V., 1978, 'Inflation, real tax revenue and the case for inflationary finance: Theory with an application to Argentina', *IMF Staff Papers*, 25, 3, 417-451.
Zanias G., 1991, 'Adjustment costs, production functions and capital-labour substitution in Greek manufacturing 1958-80', *Applied Economics*, 23, 49-55.

Index

ABOUT THE AUTHORS

Nicos Christodoulakis is Minister of Development and Professor in the Athens University of Economics. He has previously served as Deputy Minister of Finance, Economic Advisor to the Prime Minister, and Secretary General for Research and Technology. He has published extensively on economic policy, business cycles, growth, forecasting and economic models. His recent books include "*The NewLandscape of Growth*" (1998), and "*Growth and Business Cycles in Greece and the EU*" (1997).

Sarantis Kalyvitis, is Assistant Professor in the Athens University of Economics. He has worked extensively on the impact of Structural Funds on growth and has published many articles in various academic journals in the areas of international finance, growth, European structural policies, and applied econometrics.

GPSR Compliance

The European Union's (EU) General Product Safety Regulation (GPSR) is a set of rules that requires consumer products to be safe and our obligations to ensure this.

If you have any concerns about our products, you can contact us on ProductSafety@springernature.com

In case Publisher is established outside the EU, the EU authorized representative is:

Springer Nature Customer Service Center GmbH
Europaplatz 3
69115 Heidelberg, Germany

Batch number: 10704043

Printed by Printforce, the Netherlands